Hypnosis for Overthinking

The Meditation and Hypnotherapy Guide for Better Life.
Relaxation to Reclaim Your Life and Rewire Your Brain.
Relieve Stress and Overcome Worries.

HYPNOSIS FOR
OVERTHINKING

COPYRIGHT

CONTENTS

INTRODUCTION

Overthinking Disorder - What right?

Overthinking Disorder doesn't exist. There are a wide range of sorts of uneasiness disorders where an individual takes part in overthinking or rumination, yet there isn't a disorder. When an individual can't quit fixating and stressing over things it can meddle with your personal satisfaction.

You might be pondering "what conditions cause overthinking?" Some emotional well-being analyze where an individual can't prevent their mind from rumination are PTSD, injury, agoraphobia, alarm disorder, particular mutism, partition tension disorder, social nervousness disorder, fears, substance-initiated uneasiness disorders, or it might be an indication of some different sickness.

When it comes to uneasiness disorders, a considerable lot of them have overthinking as an indication. For instance, an individual with alarm disorder may ruminate and overthink when they will have a fit of anxiety once more. They fixate on something that could trigger their assault. In addition to the fact that they are on edge, they presently have meta-nervousness, which is tension about being on edge. Overthinking their fit of anxiety caused it to feel all the more overwhelming.

Overthinking is normal. You don't must have a nervousness disorder to take part in consistent rumination. You may state it's a piece of the human condition. We as a whole overthink things now and again: You might be excessively worried about what you said or did to someone. You might be stressed over performing at school or work. You may be worried about how others see you. These are on the whole instances of how you may participate in overthinking.

Different instances of overthinking include:

- When you are fixating on what you ought to have said or done
- Performance tension, or stressing over how you match others at work
- Engaging in "imagine a scenario in which" situations where you consider what could occur in an assortment of conditions.
- Catastrophizing or thinking the most exceedingly terrible will occur
- Worrying about having a fit of anxiety startlingly
- Intrusive or over the top considerations

Overthinking is inescapable, yet there's assistance for the condition. Numerous individuals experience the ill effects of fixating and agonizing over things that are out of their control. A typical treatment for this sort of uneasiness is Cognitive Behavior Therapy (CBT). CBT assists individuals with testing their negative or silly reasoning and change their contemplations into beneficial, positive ones. Getting treatment or guiding for uneasiness can have an immense effect for somebody with overthinking. You can work with a specialist in your neighborhood, with one of the prepared psychological wellness experts here at BetterHelp. Internet guiding is an incredible work environment on nervousness and begin getting the hang of adapting abilities to oversee it.

Overthinking

Numerous individuals know about the term nervousness disorder (and, truth be told, a large number of Americans experience the ill effects of a type of uneasiness disorder each day), yet we will in general neglect a significant side effect of tension disorders, which is overthinking.

The meaning of overthinking is to ruminate or fixate on something. Many individuals, when hearing this definition, may accept they are overthinkers. Who doesn't go a solitary day without overthinking something? We wonder if we're settling on the correct decisions from little things like picking the quickest course on our drive that morning or choosing the correct eatery for supper to things like our kids' prosperity and our family's wellbeing and security. Be that as it may, that is typical. It's entirely expected to stress and overthink somewhat.

In any case, there are destructive impacts overthinking can have on an individual intellectually and inwardly. When overthinking in accordance with a tension disorder, it would be extreme contemplations about something that causes one uneasiness, stress, dread, or fear. It's not simply considering something-it's fixating on something so much that it influences one's capacity to work in their life.

When you marvel or stress over yourself, your life, your family, your companions, or whatever else and you don't have an overthinking issue, whatever you're contemplating about l stresses you for some time, then after a brief timeframe, you go on with your day. You keep stressing on occasion, yet you don't continually ruminate. You don't discover the stress meddling with the remainder of your life. With overthinking as the aftereffect of a tension disorder, in any case, the stress is all the individual can consider and despite the fact that they may not fixate on something very similar constantly, they're constantly worried about something.

If you trust you may experience the ill effects of overthinking because of uneasiness, you may have discovered that you've encountered at least one of these circumstances:

- Difficulty tracking and adding to a discussion because you go over potential reactions or proclamations consistently until the discussion has either finished or the fateful opening for talking was lost
- Continually contrasting yourself with the individuals around you and how you match them
- Focusing on most pessimistic scenario situations either including yourself or the ones you love
- Reliving past disappointments or errors again and again and you can't move past them
- Worrying about future errands as well as objectives until they feel practically difficult to achieve

- Reliving a past horrible encounter, (for example, misuse or the passing of a friend or family member) leaving you incapable to adapt to it
- A failure to hinder the dashing of dubious contemplations, stresses or feelings

No two individuals will encounter overthinking similarly. In any case, the individuals who do encounter it will all find that their personal satisfaction is undermined by their failure to successfully control pessimistic musings and feelings. It can make it progressively difficult to go out and mingle, appreciate pastimes, or be gainful at fill in as their brain invests a lopsided measure of time and vitality on specific lines of thought. There's a feeling that they don't have full command over their own personalities or feelings, which can be harming to one's emotional well-being.

Causing companions or keeping them to can be difficult with overthinking because you battle to impart when something isn't right or you may convey unnecessarily. It very well may be amazingly difficult to converse with them because you're worried about what to state or to do anything with them because you're excessively worried about how you'll do or what will occur. Somebody who overthinks may battle even to continue general discussions or to collaborate in an ordinary domain. They may experience issues in any event, heading off to the store or to an arrangement.

Actually, overthinking can influence everything without exception about your life. It can influence the way you way you work with others, sway your public activity, and negatively affect your own life. This means it can begin to erode at you and at the connections you have with the individuals around you. Overthinking can make significant issues in your life.

Step by step instructions to Stop Overthinking

"Quit overthinking things!"

You may have heard this multiple occasions, and it's very unhelpful. You can't simply flip a switch and quit overthinking. Actually, being advised to quit overthinking often winds up with you thinking things more. It's an endless loop.

Basically, showing yourself not to overthink is a long procedure that you need to prepare your cerebrum to do. How about we take a gander at some normal reasons why you may overthink and instruct how to quit overthinking.

A sleeping disorder Overthinking

When you can't rest, your brain can race and you may have over the top considerations about getting rest. Often, this overthinking comes when a sleeping disorder strikes, and afterward proceeds with the following day. You may feel tired, and your mind is less engaged. You may have negative contemplations and over the top musings about not having the option to rest.

Sleep deprivation is known as an endless loop on purpose. When you have it, it's difficult to quit overthinking about not dozing. Here are a couple of ways you can lessen that when you're experiencing difficulty dozing.

Reflection and care applications. These assist you with living at the present minute, disposing of any considerations or feelings you may have that are nosy. Other than the way that care can prepare your cerebrum, it can quiet you down and make it simpler to rest.

Get up if you can't nod off. If you're sleeping and you can't nod off, it has an inclination that it's difficult to drop. Your mind connects your cerebrum with fretfulness. Get out and accomplish something unwinding. Try not to invest energy in online networking or accomplish something animating. Rather, loosen up yourself.

Understand that you're not going to pass on from the absence of rest. While your dread and nervousness discloses to you that you can't nod off, most cases are transitory. While your health decays from incessant lack of sleep, stressing a lot over an incidental episode of a sleeping disorder is going to aggravate the issue. If the issue endures, it's an ideal opportunity to see a specialist or advisor.

Basic leadership

Another motivation behind why individuals overthink is because of basic leadership. In some cases, the choice is something important. Different occasions, the basic leadership is over something somewhat senseless, for example, what eatery to pick.

While you should consider your choices, overthinking them just slows down time, particularly if you have many individuals sitting tight for you to settle on the choice. Here's the means by which to at long last defeat basic leadership uneasiness.

Settle on a period limit on your basic leadership. Presently, this time limit doesn't need to be short to the point that you feel very hurried, yet it ought to be sufficiently short to help quit overthinking.

Many individuals, particularly the major leaders, plan their reasoning occasions and wind up diverting themselves in the in the interim. Having certain occasions to think can forestall overthinking nervousness.

Once more, care and living right now can help. The present minute ought to include the rationale behind settling on the choice, not the unjustifiable feelings of trepidation you may have.

Bipolar Disorder and Overthinking

When one considers bipolar disorder, they will in general think about the psychological well-being data they think about. What's more, that health data is the way that bipolar disorder individuals will in general be either discouraged or hyper. Individuals with it make some hard memories with their state of mind, however they may likewise make some hard memories with overthinking.

With bipolar disorder, overthinking upsetting or troubling contemplations can occur with the two sides of the coin. With despondency, one might be stressed over what will occur later on. Or then again, they may stress over the symptoms of the drug they take.

With lunacy, you may experience difficulty focusing on your musings, making it harder to challenge your contemplations. It's difficult to once in a while separate the genuine from the fiction. Or on the other hand, you might be so euphoric you invest energy spending so as to have a sense of security, then think twice about it.

With bipolar disorder, it's significant you look for the assistance of online treatment or an in-person specialist. Online treatment works particularly well for gentle to direct cases. A specialist can give you the essential data and psychological wellness data about bipolar disorder. What's more, it's significant you focus on your considerations.

Now and again, your bipolar scenes can keep going for different timeframes, and your contemplations can exacerbate them. You may concentrate on the negative and cause your disorder to decline for significant stretches of times. Bipolar disorder or not, our musings that fly into our brains will in general aggravate the issue. Look for help if you need it.

Thinking Positive Thoughts

You may think about how to quit overthinking. One route is to think progressively positive musings. You may feign exacerbation at this. You're feeling that positive musings, are by definition, something that is straight out of a gooey health book.

In any case, the science backs up that positive musings and increasingly positive reasoning examples are the way to progress. If you need to think all the more emphatically, here are a few different ways to do as such.

Investigate your affirmation predisposition. Negative musings will in general wait, and when it comes to positive contemplations, it's typically the inverse. You should attempt to change that deduction around a piece.

Rather, begin to see your positive considerations. When you begin thinking decidedly, record it. Notice when you're thinking positive contemplations and aggregate them all.

We feel compelled to pressure this as much as possible. Practice care. Careful procedures instructs you to relinquish any passionate trouble. A damaging idea experiences the window. Concentrate on the positive contemplations.
Think about all the occasions you've been helping individuals. Consider something that fulfills you. Any troubling considerations, simply let them go. It is a stage procedure that requires practice.
A few people imagine that constructive reasoning methods no pessimistic reasoning at all. Anything concerning ought to be disregarded, regardless of how large it is. This isn't valid in any way. Thinking positive musings just methods having more positive speculation in the overthinking division. Troubling considerations will occur, yet positive reasoning instructs us that the enthusiastic misery is transitory and there is a great deal to consider that is sure.
Give tidying up your feed a shot internet based life. Take out the more pessimistic individuals and concentrate on energy. Indeed, you should devour pessimistic news as well, however numerous individuals are over-burden with it, and if you're an overthinker, it's bad for you.
Intellectually Strong People

Intellectually resilient individuals are less inclined to overthink. Think about your cerebrum as a muscle. The more you train it, the more intellectually solid you'll get. Expanding your emotional wellness quality is particularly significant as you age. Emotional wellness decreases with maturing, however with the correct health data, you can prepare your brain.

Here is some acceptable emotional wellness data for your psyche:

Intellectually resilient individuals practice a ton. When you consider work out, you may envision resilient individuals improving your body. Be that as it may, practice has numerous positive symptoms for your psyche. For instance, your cerebrum discharges feel-great synthetic concoctions that murder agony and help decrease your pressure hormones. Also, practice occupies you from your contemplations, making it extraordinary if you need to realize how to quit overthinking.

Intellectually resilient individuals attempt to associate as much as they can. Have a go at conversing with a dear companion and contact them on a more profound level. If you don't have any companions to converse with, take a stab at getting out and conversing with somebody in a book shop, bistro, or somewhere else. When you're conversing with new individuals and attempting to make companions, you're encountering significantly less stressing and additionally being aware of everything.

Intellectually tough individuals routinely practice subjective social treatment. This kind of treatment causes you dispose of negative behavior patterns and contemplations, and it very well may be utilized to treat a wide range of psychological sickness. Dietary problems, bipolar disorder, summed up tension disorder, and then some.

Tough individuals will in general train themselves intellectually by blending it up. Doing likewise things again and again can have some negative reactions. Take a gander at a part of your life and consider what you can do any other way. Take a stab at having another pastime, going for your fantasy work, or simply gaining some new useful knowledge. When you begin living for another day, it assists with your overthinking.

Resilient individuals will in general understand that there will be seasons of shortcoming. There are times where you invest an excessive amount of energy thinking, and afterward you notice yourself overthinking. It will occur, and you can't overthink overthinking. Now and then, it occurs. Simply don't go through hours on it. You can plan an opportunity to let your brain meander about a specific issue, and when that time is up, quit contemplating it. This is something that may take practice, however tough individuals can give it attempt.

Decrease Stress

You may ask why "decrease pressure" is on here. Indeed, stress and our propensity to overthink go connected at the hip. Stress is our body's approach to help us when we're in a tight spot in a circumstance that compromises us, nonetheless, our body can't differentiate between genuine peril and regular issues, and hence the pressure heaps on.

Individuals will in general think that its difficult to adapt to all their pressure.

Some pressure can be acceptable. Stress related with positive brain science, which is acceptable pressure, will in general test you and make you need to improve. However, positive brain research just goes up until now. An excess of stress can exacerbate your issues, including:

Making you dread dismissal, blame, disappointment, or losing everything.

You will in general stress over the things you can't change. A great many people understand that they should stress over the things they can change and disregard the things they can't change, yet it's difficult to manage overthinking that.

Physical pressure is an issue with a lot of pressure. Regular damages, truly. Physical pressure implies that pressure has genuine, excruciating impacts. Instances of physical pressure incorporate migraines and other body hurts, which may likewise be clinical gloom.

Stress can transpire. It doesn't make a difference if you're a youngster, in your teenager years, or a grown-up. If you have a propensity for overthinking and have worry, here are some basic approaches to lessen pressure. Anybody can do these straightforward ways, and these basic ways don't require a specialist, either.

Practice intellectual conduct treatment. This is something that takes practice, yet figuring out how to identify considerations that are by definition, meddling, and figuring out how to adapt to these contemplations are significant.

Record your issues and request them from most to least significant. A piece of critical thinking includes you taking care of the simplest issue first and proceeding onward up. Before long, you'll discover critical thinking simple.

Think about your dread of disappointment and other ordinary feelings of trepidation. For what reason do you dread this? How does your pressure affect you? Do you dread blame, disappointment, or something else?

Individuals don't understand the benefit of working out. It can help decrease your worry by quire a piece.

Set aside some effort to loosen up. See what's going on your preferred show. Try not to invest a lot of energy dawdling, yet rather enjoy a reprieve and return with a new personality.

Try not to consume medications or liquor. If conversing with a specialist or therapist drives them to endorse medicine, take that.

At long last, take a stab at working with a guide. They might have the option to assist you with your issues.

Neurosis

Another piece of overthinking and of summed up nervousness disorder by and large is despondency. This is when you generally feel you have something medicinally amiss with them, making it a major issue with overthinking.

There are a few people who are somewhat anxious person. For example, you may think something isn't right with you, for the most part subsequent to visiting Dr. Google, so you converse with your primary care physician. Then, you find that nothing isn't right and it's only an issue with overthinking, blended in with a touch of summed up nervousness disorder.

In any case, you might be an outrageous masochist. You are continually meeting today with your PCP about something. After you converse with your primary care physician, you despite everything have those sentiments, and no measure of conversation with your PCP appears to cause them to leave. Regardless of the amount you attempt, you despite everything believe you're wiped out.

This is something you have to look for help about. You may have something other than summed up nervousness disorder. By getting treatment, you can at last summon the mental fortitude to concede that you're fine.

Look for Motivation

While numerous individuals are incredulous about inspirational orator, they might have the option to help. Perusing tales about a man who had the option to beat tension and live or individuals who figured out how to begin living at a more seasoned age can move you and is a decent method to occupy you from your overthinking.

It's a decent method to get some psychological wellness data on an individual level. While a portion of this psychological wellness data may not be a piece of contemporary brain science, some merit looking at.

CAUSES OF OVERTHINKING

In spite of the fact that some proof proposes ladies are bound to be overthinkers than men, everybody overthinks once in a while.

Overthinking is a typical issue I address in my treatment office. Individuals often go to their arrangements making statements like, "I can't unwind. It resembles my cerebrum won't shut off," or "I can't quit contemplating how my life could have been exceptional if I'd done things any other way."

The connection among overthinking and psychological well-being issues is a chicken-or-egg type question. Overthinking is connected to mental issues, similar to gloom and tension.

Almost certainly, overthinking makes psychological wellness decay and as your emotional wellness decreases, the more probable you are to overthink. It's a horrible descending winding.

Be that as it may, it's difficult to perceive that winding when you're trapped in it. Indeed, your mind may attempt to persuade you that stressing and ruminating is some way or another accommodating.

All things considered, won't you build up a superior arrangement or keep yourself from committing a similar error if you invest more energy thinking? Not really.

Indeed, the inverse is often valid. Investigation loss of motion is a genuine issue. The more you think, the more terrible you feel. What's more, your sentiments of wretchedness, uneasiness, or outrage may cloud your judgment and keep you from making positive move.

Two Forms of Overthinking

Overthinking comes in two structures; ruminating about the past and stressing over what's to come.

It's different than critical thinking. Critical thinking includes contemplating an answer. Overthinking includes harping on the issue.

Overthinking is likewise different than self-reflection. Healthy self-reflection is tied in with getting the hang of something important to you or increasing another point of view about a circumstance. It's deliberate.

Overthinking includes harping on how awful you feel and contemplating all the things you have no influence over. It won't assist you with growing new understanding.

The difference between critical thinking, self-reflection, and overthinking isn't about the measure of time you spend in profound idea. Time spent creating inventive arrangements or gaining from your conduct is profitable. Be that as it may, time spent overthinking, regardless of whether it's 10 minutes or 10 hours, won't improve your life.

Signs You're an Overthinker

When you become progressively mindful of your inclination to overthink things, you can find a way to change. On the whole, you need to perceive that overthinking accomplishes more damage than anything else.

Some of the time, individuals imagine that their overthinking some way or another keeps terrible things from occurring. What's more, they think if they don't stress enough or repeat the past enough then by one way or another, they'll experience more issues. Be that as it may, the exploration is quite clear- -overthinking is awful for you and it does nothing to forestall or take care of issues.

Here are 10 signs that you're an overthinker:

I remember humiliating minutes in my mind over and again.

I experience difficulty resting because it feels like my mind won't shut off.

I solicit myself a great deal from "what if..." questions.

I invest a great deal of energy contemplating the shrouded importance in things individuals state or occasions that occur.

I go over discussions I had with individuals in my psyche and consider all the things I wished I had or hadn't said.

I continually remember my missteps.

When somebody says or acts in a manner I don't care for, I continue replaying it in my psyche.

At times I'm not mindful of what's happening around me because I'm harping on things that occurred previously or agonizing over things that may occur later on.

I invest a ton of energy stressing over things I have no influence over.

I can't get my psyche off my stresses.

Step by step instructions to Deal With Overthinking

If you perceive that you will in general become involved with overthinking, don't surrender. You can find a way to recover your time, vitality, and intellectual competence.

From booking time to stress to changing the channel, there are a few mental quality activities that can assist you with halting overthinking everything.

We are generally researchers.

We might not have built up course book speculations of our own and we may not rank in indistinguishable classifications from genuine and popular mathematicians, however we have all explored different avenues regarding our contemplations. We are thought researchers.

Overthinking is torment. To be secured your brain with a consistent cluster of disturbing contemplations is damnation.

How you do get away?

The cerebrum is dubious, to quit considering something, you need to consider not contemplating it trying to consider something different. It is despondent. I am maybe an interminable overthinker. I state so because I do it practically regular and it doesn't help that I am an author. Overthinking is a piece of the equation of getting a story onto paper. In any case, I have scholarly and I am as yet figuring out how to escape my head and settle my brain of these idea floods. I am figuring out how to leave the research center and show restraint about my discoveries.

The Reason:

We overthink because we are edgy animals chasing for answers. We like conviction and we like being in charge. Try not to stress, its piece of human endurance strategy. All things considered, to some degree. Overthinking isn't all terrible. Likelihood hypothesis necessitates that every conceivable result of an occasion must be investigated to figure out what can truly occur in that given circumstance.

We comprehend what that resembles; before a major occasion we end up speculation about it so much, we make theoretical beginnings and endings and even peaks of said occasion before it even occurs. As it were, it is arrangement, so we can manage whatever result there is and not experience the ill effects of an over the top astonishing outcome. What's more, in a way it is vaticination. We can't anticipate the future, yet there is a profound yearning within us that desires we could have.

Our instinct gives us half capacity to do that. Along these lines, we once in a while can detect when something isn't right, where we ought to or ought not go, who we can and can't trust. We have a ground-breaking inside voice us that can here and there spare our lives. Overthinking puts that voice on impact. It is a cruel procedure to experience yet it is in some cases vital.

The Detriment:

Overthinking is dread. Dread is a seed of a slippery tree. We were not brought into the world with dread, it happened upon us either through bestowed exercise, life experience or injury. Shockingly, we had practically zero authority over what was educated or done to us in the long periods of our youth. A considerable lot of us despite everything have parts of dread living inside us from since the times of our childhood. Things transpire in youth, connections, fellowships and in employments and the terrible piece of the encounters hook on to us so tight, the contemplations about these past encounters surface like settled toxic substance overflowing through the mind in a solitary snapshot of "thinking excessively".

We structure these ruinous idea designs that are practically inevitable once we start. We contemplate something that may be a totally guiltless circumstance, however it is because the toxic substance has emitted and penetrated our brains, we make this hellfire. The more we overthink, the more dread we welcome in and the all the more agitating our musings become. It is an endless loop particularly to the individuals who experience the ill effects of tension disorder, gloom and even self-destructive contemplations.

The most effective method to Stop:

It is difficult to totally delete dread. You can't simply "let go of dread". Reflection will assist you with quieting your contemplations and create examples of more clear reasoning yet you will always be unable to eradicate dread. Why? Because dread is a piece of human sense and it is important in that part of endurance and keeping away from peril.

Be that as it may, once in a while or maybe never will we wind up before a tiger, and we need to settle on the choice to either flee or turn into its feast. Dread then, has the ability to outmaneuver the well evolved creature or even murder it.

Stress and passionate dread is different. Dread that assaults our feelings is more diligently to class as a dread that is helping us endure. In this way, everything we do is overthink. We surrender to that kind of dread and it focuses on the mind to the point of mindlessness and now and again, craziness.

How would you stop?

Focus. Train yourself and your psyche to be increasingly mindful. I have stickers on my vision board in my workspace that says "know" and "remain centered" and as paltry as that technique appears, it makes a difference. The minute you feel yourself going to drift off into "overthinking land", you can complete two things; either be totally quiet or begin talking.

When you quiet yourself you get ready for the toxic substance, you know its coming so you prepare. Peruse, stare at the television, do errands, shower and cook. Anything will fill in as an interruption when you are quiet. Attempt to advise yourself that you are overthinking and that it will pass. Give yourself the insistence that it is dread and stress assaulting you and that you will crush it. Be solid in your quiet and show restraint for the unsettledness to alleviate.

When you begin talking you allow yourself to allow worry to. Be that as it may, be cautious, venting can be penitent, particularly when the individual or people to whom you are addressing may not get you or identify right away. Concede that you are overthinking and that you are lost in the difficulty. When you talk about what's at the forefront of your thoughts recall that it won't totally sound good to you, let alone to the individual you're conversing with. In any case, moving things out into the open immediately is a decent strategy to adjust with the goal that you don't languish over an extensive stretch alone in your mind.

Cry. Crying is recuperating. In the entirety of my grown-up years up until this point, I found that crying has helped me move past the hardest of times I have ever confronted. When I overthink I consequently get passionate and defenseless, so I wind up crying. It is agonizing and it is debilitating yet the result is conciliating. Overthinking is now a jug of prisoned musings slamming to turn out, when you cry you permit yourself to reduce a portion of the weight that accompanies being stuck inside your head. You at any point saw that migraine that comes in the wake of crying? It is a weight discharge.

If you are not an individual effortlessly brought to tears or maybe you are not yet 100% agreeable in your feelings, it will be difficult for you to simply attempt to change your grieved musings. All things considered, you first need to figure out how to associate with your feelings and your actual self.

Think. Allow me to clarify. To quit overthinking you have to think? Indeed. Because the majority of the occasions we are overthinking we are not even helpfully thinking but instead we are floundering those well used musings about our feelings of trepidation and dissatisfactions. Productive reasoning can completely change you. For the present, I'll disclose to you how it can assist with halting overthinking. We have the ability to change the manner in which we think; however it requires practice and a huge amount of self-restraint yet it isn't unimaginable.

Productive reasoning is fundamentally a perspective helpfully about your reality and condition. So as opposed to responding to these occasions, you decide to decipher and afterward react to them in manners that will bolster your development and advancement and limit contact with the outside condition. Remember that how you decipher occasions and conditions adequately decides how you will react to them inwardly.

You may not generally have the option to inform when you are concerning to overthink however you can set yourself up. You can rehearse productive reasoning. It won't be anything but difficult to do something besides sit and endure in your contemplations yet you need to discover the will help yourself first. Rather than gazing vacantly at nothing in particular and heaping your contemplations one over the out of this world, read. Perusing empowers helpful reasoning because you naturally change your consideration regarding different material that won't just shift your concentration from your harmful musings however advantage you by nourishing you information or engaging your brain.

You should recall that it is alright to overthink. It is human. Be that as it may, overthinking can demolish your life. It has caused my life much torment previously and still a few days in the present. I am as yet figuring out how to receive the previously mentioned approaches to profit my psyche. I realize that once I focus on a superior life and to better perspectives I can come back to the lab. Also, rather than testing my contemplations like rodents and purple and blue poisonous substances, I can gain proficiency with the genuine mathematician way, and follow these fitter strategies to quit overthinking. I may not ideal the science to annihilate overthinking always however with this methodology I can get closer to a healthier and more joyful personality that withstands even the cruel and dreadful conditions.

HOW TO OVERCOME OVERTHINKING

You at long last have a couple of calm minutes to yourself, possibly to quickly begin thinking about whether you neglected to send that thank-you email or whether you've overestimated your odds of getting the advancement.

Sound natural? Stressing and overthinking are a piece of the human experience, however when left unchecked, they can negatively affect your prosperity. Harping on similar contemplations may even build your danger of certain emotional wellness conditions, as per a 2013.

All in all, what's an overthinking individual to do? These tips can assist you with moving the correct way.

Venture back and see how you're reacting

The manner in which you react to your contemplations can now and again keep you in a pattern of rumination, or monotonous reasoning.

Whenever you wind up persistently running things over in your brain, observe how it influences your mind-set. Do you feel bothered, anxious, or blameworthy? What's the essential feeling behind your contemplations?

Having mindfulness is critical to changing your mentality.

Discover an interruption

Close down overthinking by including yourself in an action you appreciate.

This appears to be unique for everybody, except thoughts include:

learning some new kitchen abilities by handling another formula

heading off to your preferred exercise class

taking up another diversion, for example, painting

volunteering with a neighborhood association

It very well may be difficult to begin something new when you're overpowered by your considerations. If finding an interruption feels overwhelming, take a stab at putting aside a little piece of time — state, 30 minutes — each other day. Utilize this opportunity to either investigate potential interruptions or fiddle with existing ones.

Take a full breath

You've heard it a million times, however that is because it works. Whenever you wind up hurling and turning over your musings, close your eyes and inhale profoundly.

Attempt it

Here's a decent starter exercise to assist you with loosening up with your breath:

Locate an agreeable spot to sit and loosen up your neck and shoulders.

Spot one hand over your heart and the different over your midsection.

Breathe in and breathe out through your nose, focusing on how your chest and stomach move as you relax.

Take a stab at doing this activity three times each day for 5 minutes, or whenever you have hustling considerations.

Ponder

Building up a normal reflection practice is a proof sponsored approach to help away from brain of anxious gab by turning your consideration internal.

Not certain how to begin? We have all that you have to know right now manage. All you need is 5 minutes and a tranquil spot.

Take a gander at the master plan

By what means will all the issues skimming around in your mind influence you 5 or quite a while from now? Will anybody truly mind that you purchased a natural product plate for the potluck as opposed to preparing a pie without any preparation?

Try not to let minor issues transform into significant obstacles.

Accomplish something pleasant for another person

Attempting to facilitate the heap for another person can assist you with placing things in context. Consider ways you can be of administration to somebody experiencing a difficult time.

Does your companion who's in a separation need a couple of long periods of childcare? Would you be able to get staple goods for your neighbor who's been wiped out?

Acknowledging you have the ability to fill somebody's heart with joy better can shield negative contemplations from dominating. It additionally gives you something beneficial to concentrate on rather than your ceaseless stream of contemplations.

Perceive programmed negative reasoning

Mechanized negative contemplations (ANTs) allude to automatic negative considerations, as a rule including apprehension or outrage, you some of the time have in response to a circumstance.

Handling ANTs

You can identify and work through your ANTs by tracking your contemplations and effectively attempting to transform them:

Utilize a scratch pad to follow the circumstance giving you tension, your state of mind, and the principal felt that comes to you naturally.

As you dive into subtleties, assess why the circumstance is causing these negative musings.

Separate the feelings you're encountering and attempt to identify what you're educating yourself concerning the circumstance.

Locate an option in contrast to your unique idea. For instance, rather than hopping directly to, "This will be an epic disappointment," take a stab at something along the lines of, "I'm really trying my best."

Recognize your triumphs

When you're amidst overthinking, stop and take out your scratch pad or your preferred note-taking application on your telephone. Scribble down five things that have gone directly over the previous week and your job in them.

These don't should be gigantic achievements. Perhaps you adhered to your espresso spending this week or wiped out your vehicle. When you see it on paper or on-screen, you may be shocked at how these easily overlooked details include.

If it feels accommodating, allude back to this rundown when you discover your contemplations spiraling.

Remain present

Not prepared to focus on a contemplation schedule? There are a lot of different approaches to ground yourself right now.

Think about different perspectives

At times, calming your musings requires venturing outside of your typical point of view. How you see the world is molded by your life encounters, qualities, and suppositions. Envisioning things from a different perspective can assist you with working through a portion of the commotion.

Scribble down a portion of the contemplations whirling around in your mind. Attempt to explore how legitimate everyone is. For instance, possibly you're worrying about an up and coming excursion because you simply realize it will be a catastrophe. In any case, is that actually what will occur? What sort of evidence do you need to back that up?

Make a move

Here and there, you may go over similar contemplations more than once because you aren't taking any solid activities about a specific circumstance.

Can't quit considering somebody you envy? Rather than having it ruin your day, let your emotions assist you with settling on better decisions.

Whenever you're visited by the green-peered toward beast, be proactive and write down ways you can approach arriving at your objectives. This will get you out of your head and channel your vitality into making noteworthy strides.

Practice self-empathy

Harping on past slip-ups shields you from giving up. If you're thrashing yourself over something you did a week ago, give pulling together a shot self-sympathy.

Here are a few different ways to kick you off:

Observe a distressing idea.

Focus on the feelings and real reactions that emerge.

Recognize that your emotions are valid for you at the time.

Embrace an expression that addresses you, for example, "May I acknowledge myself as I am" or "I am sufficient."

Grasp your feelings of dread

A few things will consistently be out of your control. Figuring out how to acknowledge this can go far toward controling overthinking.

Obviously, this is more difficult than one might expect, and it won't occur incidentally. In any case, search for little open doors where you can stand up to the circumstances you much of the time stress over. Possibly it's facing a bossy collaborator or taking that independent day trip you've been longing for.

Request help

You don't need to go only it. Looking for outside assistance from a qualified advisor can assist you with growing new devices for working through your musings and in any event, changing your attitude.

Considering something in unlimited circles — is depleting.

While everybody overthinks a couple of things now and again, incessant over-scholars invest the greater part of their waking energy ruminating, which squeezes themselves. They then slip-up that strain to be pressure.

"There are individuals who have levels of overthinking that are simply obsessive," says clinical analyst Catherine Pittman, a partner teacher in the brain science office at Saint Mary's College in Notre Dame, Indiana.

"Be that as it may, the normal individual additionally simply tends to overthink things." Pittman is likewise the creator of "Revamp Your Anxious Brain: How to Use the Neuroscience of Fear to End Anxiety, Panic, and Worry."

Overthinking can take numerous structures: unendingly thinking when settling on a choice (and afterward scrutinizing the choice), endeavoring to understand minds, attempting to anticipate the future, adding something extra to the littlest of subtleties, and so on.

Individuals who overthink reliably run critiques in their minds, reprimanding and dismantling what they said and did yesterday, terrified that they look awful — and worrying about an awful future that may anticipate them

'What ifs' and 'shoulds' command their speculation, as though an imperceptible jury is sitting in judgment on their lives. Furthermore, they likewise obsess about what to post online because they are profoundly worried about how others will decipher their posts and updates.

They don't rest soundly because ruminating and stressing keep them conscious around evening time. "Ruminators redundantly go over occasions, posing large inquiries: Why did that occur? What does it mean?" includes Susan Nolen-Hoeksema, the seat of the division of brain research at Yale University and the creator of Women Who Think Too Much: How to Break Free of Overthinking and Reclaim Your Life. "However, they never discover any answers."

If you reliably center around ruminating and make it a propensity, it turns into a circle, And the more you do it, the harder it is to stop. Clinical therapist Helen Odessky, Psy. D., shares some understanding. "So often individuals mistake overthinking for critical thinking," says Odessky, the creator of "Prevent Anxiety from Stopping You." "Yet what winds up happening is we simply kind of go in a circle," Odessky says. "We're not so much taking care of an issue."

Overthinking is damaging and intellectually depleting. It can cause you to feel like you're stuck in one spot, and if you don't act, it can enormously affect on your everyday life. It can immediately put your health and all out prosperity in danger. Rumination makes you increasingly powerless to misery and nervousness.

Numerous individuals overthink because they are terrified of things to come, and what might turn out badly. "Because we feel helpless about the future, we continue attempting to tackle issues in our mind," says David Carbonell, a clinical analyst and creator of "The Worry Trick: How Your Brain Tricks You into Expecting the Worst and What You Can Do About It."

Extraordinary overthinking can undoubtedly sap your feeling of power over your life. It denies us of dynamic cooperation in everything around us.

"Ceaseless worriers show an expanded rate of coronary issues and stifled invulnerable working. Choosing not to move on or the future likewise removes us from the present, rendering us incapable to finish the work as of now on our plates. If you ask ruminators how they are feeling, none will say "cheerful." Most feel hopeless," says Nicholas Petrie, a senior employee at the Center for Creative Leadership.

Overthinking can trap the cerebrum in a stress cycle. When ruminating become as normal as breathing, you have to rapidly manage it and discover an answer for it.

"When an undesirable occasion sets us feeling dejected, it's simpler to review different occasions when we've felt horrendous. That can make way for a ruminator to work herself into a descending winding," composes Amy Maclin of Real Simple.

Instructions to vanquish this example of reasoning and win your life back

Incessant stressing isn't perpetual. It's a psychological propensity that can be broken. You can prepare your mind to take a gander at life from a different point of view

To defeat overthinking, Pittman prescribes you supplant the idea. "Instructing yourself to not to have a specific idea isn't the best approach to not have the idea," she says."You need to supplant the idea." What if she were to inform you to quit thinking concerning pink elephants? What are you going to think about? It's hard to believe, but it's true: pink elephants. If you would prefer not to consider a pink elephant, evoke a picture of, state, a tortoise. "Perhaps there's a major tortoise holding a rose in its mouth as it slithers," says Pittman. "You're not contemplating pink elephants now."

Work yourself out of it by seeing when you're latched onto your subconscious mind. You can tame your overthinking propensity if you can begin taking a grasp on your self-talk — that inward voice that gives a running monolog for the duration of the day and even into the night.

"You can develop a little mental separation by creating different understandings of the circumstance, which makes your negative considerations less trustworthy," says Bruce Hubbard, the chief of the Cognitive Health Group and an extra right hand teacher of brain research and training at Columbia University. This is called subjective rebuilding.

Ask yourself — What's the likelihood that what I'm terrified of will really occur? If the likelihood is low, what are some more probable results?

If it's an issue you continue ruminating about, reword the issue to mirror the positive result no doubt about it," recommends Nolen-Hoeksema.

"Rather than "I'm stuck in my profession," let yourself know or better despite everything express, "I need a vocation where I feel increasingly locked in." Then make an arrangement to grow your abilities, system, and search for open doors for a superior profession.

Locate a valuable method for preparing any stresses or negative considerations, says Honey. "Record your musings in a diary consistently before bed or before anything else — they don't need to be in any request. Do a 'cerebrum dump' of everything at the forefront of your thoughts onto the page. Once in a while that can manage the cost of a good feeling, " suggests Honey Langcaster-James, a clinician.

You can likewise control your ruminating propensity by interfacing with your faculties. Start to see what you can hear, see, smell, taste, and feel.

The thought is to reconnect with your prompt world and everything around you. When you start to see, you invest less energy in your mind.

You can likewise see your overthinking propensity and work yourself out of it. Turning out to be mindful can assist you with taking control.

"Give somewhat more consideration," says Carbonell. "State something like: I'm feeling sort of on edge and awkward. Where am I? Am I all in my mind? Possibly I ought to go for a stroll around the square and see what occurs." Perceive your mind is in overdrive or ruminating mode, and afterward attempt to wake up right away. Or on the other hand better despite everything, occupy yourself and divert your consideration regarding something different that requires center.

"If you have to hinder and supplant many times each day, it will stop quick, presumably inside a day," says Dr Margaret Weherenberg, an analyst and creator of The 10 Best-Ever Anxiety Management Techniques. "Regardless of whether the switch is essentially to return thoughtfulness regarding the job that needs to be done, it ought to be a choice to change ruminative contemplations."

It takes practice, yet with time, you will have the option to effortlessly perceive when you are stressing superfluously, and pick rather, to accomplish something, in actuality, instead of investing a ton of energy in your mind.

For instance, convert, "I can't accept this occurred" to "What would i be able to do to keep it from happening once more?" or convert "I don't have great companions!" to "What steps might I be able to take to develop the fellowships I have and find new ones?" prescribes Ryan Howes, PhD.

Try not to lose all sense of direction in musings about what you could have, would have, and ought to have done another way. Mental pressure can truly affect your personal satisfaction.

An overactive personality can make life hopeless. Figuring out how to quit investing energy in your mind is perhaps the best gift you can give yourself.

Like all propensities, changing your damaging idea examples can be a test, yet it's certainly feasible. With training, you can prepare your mind to see things differently and decrease the pressure of overthinking.

If overthinking is destroying your life, and if you figure you might be spiraling into despondency because of your considerations, it pays to get proficient assistance.

STRATEGIES TO STOP OVERTHINKING

Considerations are incredible. Your musings become your world. As Tony says, "Whatever you hold in your psyche on a predictable premise is actually what you will involvement with your life." This is something that the world's best individuals acknowledge – and the main difference among them and every other person is that they have figured out how to outfit the intensity of contemplations to enable them to accomplish.

This is likewise uplifting news for the individuals who need to realize how to quit overthinking. You weren't brought into the world an overthinker – all people have examples to their conduct. These examples create after some time dependent on life encounters. What's more, similarly as examples are found out, they can likewise be unlearned.

The key is to identify what's making you overthink, then make unequivocal move to change your mentality. Yet, that can be actually quite difficult.

WHAT IS OVERTHINKING?

The exemplary overthinking definition is, "to consider something to an extreme or for a really long time." While it's human instinct to thoroughly consider things when settling on a choice or assessing a circumstance, it becomes overthinking when you can't escape your own head. It happens to us all sooner or later in our lives – we as a whole encounter occasions that cause us stress or stress. In any case, a few people can't kill their interests. They stress over the future, making disastrous expectations about impossible occasions that haven't occurred at this point. They likewise ruminate about the past, pounding themselves about "should haves" and "could haves." They worry over what others may consider them or let negative self-talk develop in their psyches.

Overthinking an extreme choice you need to make can likewise cause issues. Replaying all the choices in your mind can prompt "loss of motion by investigation" – you're reluctant to make an inappropriate move, so you make no move by any means. In any case, in any event, settling on an inappropriate choice is superior to settling on no choice.

Regardless of whether you're an incessant overthinker or need to settle on an intense choice, you've most likely experienced restless evenings when your cerebrum just won't kill. Overthinking can build indications of gloom, raise your feelings of anxiety and cloud your judgment.

For what reason DO I OVERTHINK?

Before you can figure out how to quit overthinking, you should initially address the inquiry, "For what reason do I overthink?" Often overthinking is a result of nervousness or discouragement. If this is the situation, you may need to get your tension or wretchedness diminish overthinking. You may find that overthinking just emerges you have to settle on an extreme life choice or are managing your frailties. If overthinking isn't a side effect of a more profound intense subject matter, it can often be tended to by changing contemplations and mentalities.

The most effective method to STOP OVERTHINKING

Many individuals ask themselves "For what reason do I overthink?" and never concoct an answer. Be that as it may, stress and stress are feelings – and you can control your feelings. As Tony Robbins says, "Let dread be an advisor and not a jailor." It's a great opportunity to confront your apprehensions with the goal that you can defeat them – and attempt these seven different ways to quit overthinking everything for good.

1. Deal with YOUR STORY

Tony says, "We are altogether revealing to ourselves stories. The inquiry is, does your story enable you or keep you down?" The tales we inform ourselves regarding what our identity is sway each part of our lives. Overthinkers may let themselves know, "I've generally been a worrier" or "I'm simply normally more on edge than every other person." These are stories that keep you down and can be particularly difficult to change if you've never asked yourself "For what reason do I overthink?"

To defeat your restricting convictions, you have to initially identify them. Then you can get yourself when you begin revealing to yourself these negative stories and supplant them with positive ones, similar to "I am responsible for my feelings." Once you change your story, you'll transform you.

2. Relinquish THE PAST

Overthinkers often center around the past, exhausting vitality on "what ifs" and "should haves." Those who see how to quit overthinking realize that the past is only that. It can't be changed. The main thing you can change is the importance you provide for it. Relinquishing the past methods you don't let your errors control your future choices – and you don't let terrible things that have been done to you control your feelings. You excuse others and let go of your resentment. It's one of the most significant ways you can change your story.

3. LIVE IN THE MOMENT

Living at the time is critical to figuring out how to quit overthinking. A great many people can't simply flip a switch and live at the time – or can they? You can assume responsibility for your brain and leave negative feelings speechless. Identify overthinking before it spirals wild and pause for a moment to reset. Inhale and spotlight on the occasion – what are you hearing and seeing? What are you thankful for? From the outset, it will take cognizant mindfulness. Every day ceremonies like contemplation and preparing can assist you with retraining your cerebrum to live at the time. Before long you'll see it falls into place without a hitch.

live at the time

4. Assume Responsibility for YOUR EMOTIONS

Living at the time doesn't mean you should cover your negative feelings. So as to ace your feelings, you have to recognize them and identify their underlying drivers. When you're feeling on edge, burrow further. It's often about confronting your bigger apprehensions, for example, not feeling in charge of your life or not advancing in a manner you'd prefer to be. Become mindful of the main drivers of your overthinking and you can begin gaining ground to stop it before it begins.

5. Concentrate ON SOLUTIONS

As Tony says, "Identify your issues, yet give your capacity and vitality to arrangements." You've identified the genuine explanations behind your pressure and uneasiness, yet your work isn't finished. The best way to figure out how to quit overthinking for good is to assume responsibility for your life. If your overthinking is brought about by worry at work, reconsider your vocation way. If you're not where you need to be in life, set objectives for yourself with the goal that you can arrive. If you feel like life is out of your control, settle on a choice today to get back in the driver's seat. These are large moves, and they take guts. Keep in mind: No one controls your existence however you – don't you need your life to be phenomenal?

Concentrating on arrangements

6. Realize THE DIFFERENCE BETWEEN FEAR AND INTUITION

Overthinkers may experience difficulty recognizing the dread of committing an error, which prompts overthinking to where they settle on no choice, and a profound inclination that something isn't right. Knowing if dread or instinct is directing your conduct will assist you with escaping your head and make the following fundamental strides. By interfacing with your body, taking a couple of full breaths and truly feeling what it resembles to settle on a choice, you can translate whether dread or instinct are in play and how to best push ahead.

7. ASK YOURSELF THE RIGHT Inquiries

Asking yourself an inappropriate inquiries – including "For what reason do I overthink?" again and again – won't enable you to identify what's truly going on in your considerations or your life. They'll just encourage more overthinking. Concentrate on arrangement situated inquiries that are proactive instead of those that trigger rumination. Rather than asking "For what reason do every one of my connections go bad?" ask "What vitality am I anticipating that pulls in negative accomplices?" When you pose inquiries that permit you to make changes to your own conduct and push ahead in a healthier way, you can lessen overthinking and improve your life.

When you find how to quit overthinking and live at the time, you'll be more joyful, progressively refreshed and impact everyone around you. Continuously recollect that life occurs for you, not to you. Indeed, even your negative feelings can prompt positive results, if you treat them as a gifts that have been given to enable you to develop.

What is keeping individuals away from the life that they genuinely need to live?

I'd state that one normal and ruinous thing is that they don't have the foggiest idea how to quit overthinking.

They overthink each and every issue until it increases and more unnerving than it really is. They overthink positive things until they don't look so sure any longer (and as the tension begins to assemble).

Or then again overanalyze and deconstruct things thus the joy that originates from simply getting a charge out of something at the time vanishes.

Presently, considering things can be an extraordinary thing obviously.

Be that as it may, losing all sense of direction in a kind of overthinking disorder can bring about turning out to be somebody who stops in life. In turning out to be somebody who self-disrupts the beneficial things that occur in life.

I know. I used to overthink things a great deal and it kept me down in manners that weren't enjoyment in any way.

Yet, in the previous 10 years or so I've figured out how to make this issue so little that it once in a while springs up any longer.

What's more, if it does then I recognize what to do to defeat it.

Right now prefer to share 12 propensities that have helped me in a major, large approach to turn into a less difficult and more intelligent mastermind and to live a more joyful and less frightful life.

1. Put things into a more extensive viewpoint.

Quit Overthinking 2

Report this promotion

It's extremely simple to fall into the snare of overthinking minor things in life.

So when you are contemplating something ask yourself:

Will this issue in 5 years? Or on the other hand even in 5 weeks?
I've discovered that enlarging the viewpoint by utilizing this basic inquiry can rapidly wake up me from overthinking and help me to relinquish that circumstance.
It permits me to at long last quit contemplating something and to concentrate my time and vitality on something different that really does make a difference to me.
2. Set brief timeframe limits for choices.
If you don't have a period limit for when you should settle on a choice and make a move then you can simply continue turning your musings around and around and see them from all edges in your psyche for quite a while.
So figure out how to turn out to be better at settling on choices and to get a move on setting cutoff times in your day by day life. Regardless of if it's a little or greater choice.
This is what has worked for me:
For little choices like if ought to proceed to do the dishes, react to an email or work out I for the most part allow myself 30 seconds or less to settle on a choice.
For to some degree bigger choices that would have taken me days or weeks to thoroughly consider in the past I utilize a cutoff time for 30 minutes or for the finish of the workday.
3. Quit setting your day up for stress and overthinking.
You can't thoroughly abstain from overpowering or extremely upsetting days.

Be that as it may, you can limit the quantity of them in your month and year by getting a decent beginning to your day and by not setting yourself up for pointless pressure, overthinking and languishing.

Three things that help me with that are:

Get a decent beginning.

I've referenced this multiple occasions at this point. Also, all things considered.

Because how you start your day will in general often set the pace for your day.

A focused on morning prompts focused on day. Devouring negative data as you ride the transport to your activity will in general lead to progressively skeptical considerations during the remainder of your day.

While for instance perusing something uplifting over breakfast, getting some activity and afterward beginning with your most significant undertaking right presently establishes a decent pace for the afternoon and will assist you with staying positive.

Single-errand and take ordinary breaks.

This will assist you with keeping a sharp concentration during your day and to complete what's generally significant while likewise permitting you to rest and energize so you don't begin to barely scrapes by.

Furthermore, this to some degree loosened up outlook yet with the restricted center will assist you with thinking unmistakably and conclusively and abstain from ending up in a focused and overthinking headspace.

Limit your day by day input.

An excessive amount of data, too often of simply taking a couple of moments to check your inbox, Facebook or Twitter record or how your blog or site is doing prompts more info and mess in your psyche as your day advances.

Thus it gets more earnestly to think in a straightforward and clear manner and simpler to slip by once more into that commonplace overthinking propensity.

4. Become an individual of activity.

Quit Overthinking 3

When you realize how to begin with making a move reliably every day then you'll linger less by overthinking.

Setting cutoff times and a decent tone for the day are two things that have helped me to turn out to be substantially more of individual of activity.

Making little strides forward and just concentrating on completing each little strides in turn is another propensity that have worked truly well.

It works so well because you don't feel overpowered thus you don't need escape into tarrying or sluggish inaction.

Furthermore, despite the fact that you might be apprehensive, making only a stride is such a little thing, that you don't get incapacitated in dread.

5. Understand that you can't control everything.

Attempting to thoroughly consider things multiple times can be an approach to attempt to control everything. To cover each outcome so you don't chance committing an error, come up short or resembling a bonehead.

Be that as it may, those things are a piece of carrying on with a life where you genuinely stretch your usual range of familiarity. Everybody who you may respect and have carried on with a life that moves you has fizzled. They have committed errors.

In any case, much of the time they've additionally considered these to be as important input to gain from.

Those things that may look negative have shown them a great deal and have been priceless to assist them with growing.

So quit attempting to control everything. Attempting to do so essentially doesn't work because nobody can see every single imaginable situation ahead of time.

This is obviously more difficult than one might expect. So do it in little advances if you like.

6. State stop in a circumstance where you realize you can't think straight.

In some cases when I'm eager or when I'm lying in bed and are going to rest negative considerations begin humming around in my psyche.

In the past they could do a considerable amount of harm. These days I've gotten the hang of getting them rapidly and to state to myself:

No, no, we won't consider this now.

I realize that when I'm eager or drowsy then my psyche some of the time will in general be helpless against not thinking plainly and to pessimism.

So I follow up my "no, no... " expression and I state to myself that I will thoroughly consider this circumstance or issue when I realize that my mind will work much better.

For instance, after I've eaten something or toward the beginning of the day after I have gotten my long periods of rest.

It took a touch of training to get this to work however I've gotten quite great at delaying thinking right now. What's more, I know for a fact that when I return to a circumstance with some reasonable speculation then in 80% of the cases the issue is exceptionally little to nonexistent.

Also, if there is a main problem then my brain is set up to manage it in much better and progressively useful manner.

7. Try not to lose all sense of direction in unclear feelings of dread.

Another snare I've fallen into ordinarily that have prodded on overthinking is that I've become mixed up in unclear feelings of dread about a circumstance in my life.
Thus my mind going crazy has made catastrophe situations about what could occur if I accomplish something.
So I've figured out how to ask myself: truly, what is the most terrible that could occur?
What's more, when I've made sense of what the most terrible that could happen really is then I can likewise invest a little energy to think about what I can do if that often truly improbable thing occurs.
I've discovered that the most terrible that could practically happen is normally something that isn't as frightening as what my mind going out of control with obscure dread could create.

Discovering clearness right now just takes a couple of moments and bit of vitality and it can spare you a ton of time and languishing.
8. Work out.
This may sound somewhat odd.
However, working out can truly help with relinquishing inward strains and stresses.
It frequently causes me to feel progressively conclusive and when I was a greater amount of an overthinker then it was often my go-to strategy for changing the headspace I was in to an increasingly helpful one.

9. Get a lot of good quality rest.

Quit Overthinking

I think this is one of the most regularly disregarded components when it comes to keeping an inspirational outlook and not become mixed up in negative idea propensities.

Because when you haven't rested enough then you become increasingly defenseless.

Helpless against stressing and cynicism. To not thinking as unmistakably as you normally do. Also, to getting lost in considerations moving around and around in your brain as you overthink.

So let me share several my preferred tips that help me to rest better:

Keep it cool.

It can feel decent from the start to get into a comfortable room. In any case, I've discovered that I rest better and all the more tranquilly with less unnerving or negative dreams if I keep the room cool.

Keep the earplugs close by.

If you, similar to me, are effectively awoken by clamors then a couple basic earplugs can be a life-saver.

These reasonable things have helped me to get a decent night's rest and rest through snorers, loud felines and different aggravations a larger number of times than I can recollect.

Try not to attempt to compel yourself to rest.

If you don't feel languid then don't get into bed and attempt to compel yourself to rest.

That, at any rate I would say, just prompts hurling and turning in my bed for an hour or more.

A superior arrangement in these circumstances is to slow down for an additional 20-30 minutes on the love seat with, for instance, some perusing. This encourages me to rest quicker and, at last, get more rest.

10. Invest a greater amount of your energy right now.

By being right now in your regular day to day existence as opposed to previously or a potential future in your mind you can supplant increasingly more of the time you generally go through on overthinking things with simply being here right now.

Three different ways that I often use to reconnect with the present minute are:

Slow down.

Slow down how you do whatever you are doing well at this point. Move more slow, talk more slow or ride your bike all the more gradually for instance.

By doing so you become increasingly mindful of how you utilize your body and what's going on surrounding you at the present time.

Let yourself know: Now I am...

I often disclose to myself this: Now I am X. Furthermore, X could be brushing my teeth. Going for a stroll in the forested areas. Or then again doing the dishes.

This basic update encourages my brain to quit meandering and takes my concentration back to what's going on at this time.

Upset and reconnect.

If you believe you are losing all sense of direction in overthinking then disturb that idea by – in your psyche – yelling this to yourself : STOP!

Then reconnect with the present minute by taking only 1-2 minutes to concentrate completely on what is happening around you. Take it all in with every one of your faculties. Feel it, hear it, smell it, see it and sense it on your skin.

11. Invest a greater amount of your energy with individuals who don't overthink things.

Your social condition has a major impact.

Also, not simply the individuals and gatherings near you, all things considered. Yet in addition what you read, tune in to and watch. The sites, books, gatherings, motion pictures, webcasts and music in your life.

So consider if there are any sources in your life – close by or further away – that empowers and tends make more overthinking in your psyche. Also, consider what individuals or sources that has the contrary impact on you. Discover approaches to invest a greater amount of your energy and consideration with the individuals and info that positively affect your reasoning and less on the impacts that will in general strengthen your overthinking propensity.

12. Know about the issue (and remind yourself consistently)

Monitoring your test is critical to bring an end to the propensity for overthinking.

Be that as it may, if you're believing that you'll simply make sure to quit overthinking during your ordinary day then you're likely simply tricking yourself.

At any rate if you're in any way similar to me.

Because I required assistance. It wasn't difficult to get it however. I just made a couple of updates.

My fundamental one was a note on the whiteboard I had on one of my dividers at that point. It said "Keep things very basic".

Seeing this multiple occasions during my day helped me to wake up from overthinking quicker and to after some time incredibly limit this negative propensity.

Two different sorts of updates that you can utilize are:

A little composed note.

Essentially utilize a post-it note or something comparative and record my whiteboard expression, an inquiry like "Am I overcomplicating this?" or some other update that interests to you.

Put that note where you can't abstain from seeing it like for instance on your bedside table, your restroom reflect or next to your PC screen.

An update on your advanced mobile phone.

Record one of the expressions above or one of you claim picking in an update application on your advanced mobile phone.

I for instance utilize my Android telephone and the free application called Google Keep to do this.

HYPNOSIS FOR OVERTHINKING

Stop over-thinking and start this delicate, tolerant hypnosis session

Examination Paralysis

Vocalist lyricist Paul Simon composed an incredible tune called 'Perhaps I think excessively' which must impact anyone who invests a great deal of energy in their mind attempting to thoroughly consider everything.

You've most likely seen that investing an excess of energy thinking brings about not a great deal of doing - or in any event, being. Be that as it may, when you have in the propensity for over-thinking everything, it very well may be dubious to escape this condition of 'investigation loss of motion'.

It appears glaringly evident from the outset sight that contemplating things top to bottom and detail is a valuable activity. What else are cerebrums and psyches for? Most likely if you need to comprehend the world, you need to consider it? Most likely if you need to get individuals, and what they state and do, you need to dissect what their words and activities mean? Furthermore, obviously, this is valid - to a limited extent. Just not generally and all over.

An excessive amount of reasoning can be counterproductive

Our cerebrums have different methods for grasping and reacting to the world than systematic idea. If we don't, for reasons unknown, utilize these different methods of cognizance, and come to depend absolutely on scientific preparing, we run into the issue of unavoidable losses.

This implies, past a specific stage, the more you think, the less advantage you get. It gets counterproductive, despite the fact that it despite everything feels valuable.

The expenses of over-thinking can be high

Over-thinking in the end settles on it exceptionally difficult to take choices. An excessive amount of speculation impedes making a move. An excessive amount of reasoning can remove the heart from connections.

Indeed, even simply typical regular cooperations with others, work partners or companions or family, can turn into a minefield of vulnerability and sick inclination if an excess of stressing, analyzing and investigation goes on unchecked.

How would you approach 'altering your perspective'?

Be that as it may, regardless of whether you are completely mindful of the drawback of over-thinking, changing a since quite a while ago settled example of stress and examination can appear to be a really overwhelming test.

All things considered, your cerebrum will have gotten set in its examples of thought, and you can't simply tell it to begin carrying on differently (however no uncertainty you've attempted).

Curiously, you truly need to utilize different pieces of your cerebrum to achieve this change. The 'scientific' part itself (what they call left-cerebrum thinking) has just assumed its job by cautioning you to the presence of the issue, yet the arrangement will originate from the non-explanatory part (the correct mind).

Obviously, this left/right division is an over-simplification, yet it fills the need here.

Getting to different methods of reasoning

How would you access your non-explanatory, non-reasonable personality? It's sufficiently simple to do this by resting. Consistently, when you dream, it is the oblivious, non-sound piece of your mind which creates your fantasy life.

Dreams have been demonstrated to be the instrument by which the cerebrum builds up and keeps up instinctual reactions, and procedures the impacts of passionate excitement in the psyche/body framework.

Resting, useful for what it's worth, isn't exactly the appropriate response here, be that as it may. What's required is an approach to actuate 'dream work' in the mind, and to utilize it in the waking state. Also, the most ideal approach to do this is to utilize hypnosis.

How hypnosis can assist you with defeating investigation loss of motion

Stop Analysis Paralysis is a sound hypnosis session planned specifically to enact and use the oblivious handling intensity of your mind.

When you kick back and hear it out, you will see a kind of 'stereo' impact. That is, as a profoundly systematic individual, you will find that you know about listening scientifically from one viewpoint, and furthermore retaining another point of view comprehensively, or artificially, on the other.

This methodology has been utilized purposely in Stop Analysis Paralysis to make it simpler to 'get' the profound difference in context on life that it creates.

You will think that its both pleasant and profoundly unwinding to tune in to, and the more consistently you tune in, the more agreeable you will feel about relinquishing exorbitant investigation, while realizing that your systematic instruments stay accessible whenever they are genuinely required.

Download Stop Analysis Paralysis now and take the brakes off your life. You can tune in on your PC or gadget or through our free application which you can get to when you have finished your buy.

Do you continually fixate on things you said or ought to have said? Is it true that you are prone to envision horrible situations or results? Is it accurate to say that you are continually contrasting yourself with others? Do you stress that individuals may contemplate you when they see you out in the open, regardless of whether they don't have any acquaintance with you? This hypnosis can assist you with stopping overthinking and carry on with a loose and quiet life.

When we encounter an intricate choice or circumstance that can possibly have serious outcomes in our lives, our mind is modified to concentrate on upsides and downsides, imagining potential situations and discovering answers for potential difficulties before we even experience them. During this procedure, you may encounter tension and adrenaline discharge to keep you centered and empowered.

Present day life, be that as it may, is progressively serious and moving at an a lot quicker pace. Our physiology and brain science can decipher this bustling lifestyle as perilous or requesting. The moving drive from home to work, the several individuals you communicate with consistently or your bustling timetable can cause tension and this may prompt constant overthinking. Your mind is attempting to diminish any future dangers or potential negative outcomes, regardless of whether there isn't any.

This hypnosis plans to supplant the negative convictions you have about your circumstance with positive, practical musings and feelings. The trade happens in your subliminal personality, and can naturally wipe out overthinking and your propensity to make consider the possibility that situations in your mind.

As You Relax And Listen Repeatedly To This Stop Overthinking Hypnosis Download, You'll Notice That:

You quit fixating on things that you did and said around individuals

You quit envisioning awful results of the considerable number of choices you make

As a rule, you are getting progressively loose and content with yourself

You quit lamenting awful choices and you proceed onward with your life

Over-examining and tension can have an incredibly incapacitating impact on your satisfaction and true serenity. The following are different projects that you can look over. Download your hypnotherapy recording today.

Figure out How To Stop Analyzing Things Too Much

Overthinking and overanalyzing is an immediate consequence of tension and stress. Negative things that you intuitively accept because of past encounters or a distressing lifestyle can get installed in your subliminal personality and impact your conduct. This hypnosis comprises of a sound chronicle that you can tune in to whenever you are undisturbed and ready to give your full focus.

When you tune in to the account, it will give you a lot of straightforward directions to initiate a sleep inducing state. This is a changed perspective where you may turn out to be significantly loose and your mind's alpha wave movement increments. During this express, your cognizant personality is briefly suspended and your subliminal personality turns out to be increasingly open to sleep inducing recommendations.

Sleep inducing proposals are defined as perceptions and attestations. Its point is to address your intuitive personality straightforwardly and to supplant any antagonistic convictions, musings, or feelings you may have. Since these progressions occur in your subliminal personality, it can modify your conduct consequently and help you to quit overthinking each occasion and cooperation during your day. It can likewise assist you with stopping dreading the most noticeably terrible potential outcomes, without you effectively captivating intellectually or intentionally.

A Way To Stop Overthinking Your Life And Start Living Positively

If you tend to overthink and over break down everything, this hypnosis can assist you with becoming loose and carry on with a life that is certain and quiet. Subjectively compelling yourself to quit overthinking can be difficult since overthinking is brought about by subliminal nervousness and passionate agony. Hypnotherapy tends to the base of your over reasoning, making it a simple and charming approach to quit overthinking and overanalyzing. Hypnosis can likewise help you in different parts of your life. It can assist you with sleeping better and be increasingly beneficial during the day. It can likewise help your certainty and lessen uneasiness.

To pick up the best outcomes from this hypnosis, consistently attempt to tune in to the account whenever you are feeling loose and when you won't be upset. The best time to tune in to the hypnosis is around evening time when you are preparing for bed. If you don't see quick outcomes, recall that individuals respond differently to hypnotherapy and you may need to tune in to the chronicle on various occasions to get the ideal impact.

Start The Process Of Living A Happy, Peaceful Life Today

Tune in to this chronicle each day as a feature of your every day schedule. Hypnotherapy can be a magnificent method to quit overthinking and to assume responsibility for your uneasiness. Download your self-hypnosis recording today!

HOW HYPNOSIS CAN STOP OVERTHINKING

Many of us get somewhat on edge now and again and this is consummately normal in specific circumstances. Once in a while, in any case, restless reasoning can get ongoing, and individuals can wind up in a condition of consistent pressure and overpower.

Long haul uneasiness and stress are upsetting for the individual encountering it, but on the other hand it's awful for their health as well. Fussing, stressing and over-thinking can affect on a person's public activity, sexual coexistence and rest, just as their capacity to think obviously and decide.

For a few, endorsed prescription might be a momentary answer, however numerous individuals would prefer not to take pills, leaning toward rather to look for help to address the issue through directing, psychotherapy and progressively hypnotherapy.

Woman sitting taking a gander at water

Treatment utilizing hypnosis is a well-known decision for those looking for help for tension and frenzy, as hypnosis is just a condition of profound unwinding; a condition of serenity that very often evades the individuals who have created nervousness disorders. Hypnotherapy is additionally a 'brief treatment' which implies that outcomes can be knowledgeable about a moderately short space of time.

Individuals who are encountering nervousness are probably going to be over-thinking; going again and again genuine, envisioned or overstated apprehensions and this procedure prompts increasingly damaging reasoning. Unfortunately, restless people once in a while center around constructive contemplations or 'run motion pictures' of glad occasions in their mind. Positive contribution from others is often rejected, reduced or disposed of.

So by what method would hypnotherapy be able to help battle uneasiness or frenzy?

Indeed, aside from being a profoundly loosened up state, hypnosis can be a compelling method to change unhelpful idea examples or negative convictions. During hypnosis, our 'head babble' quietens down and our oblivious (subliminal) personality is available to constructive proposal.

Toward the finish of a loosening up session of hypnosis, customers often portray feeling lighter, more clear and ready to 'think straight'. Hypnosis isn't enchantment, yet it's an extraordinary apparatus for change. Numerous clinical subliminal specialists will likewise show self-hypnosis to their customers; self-hypnosis is an incredible route for customers to feel they have some control of their psychological state and prosperity.

There are barely any things more terrible than not feeling like yourself because of psychological wellness battles. A few people will never live through this experience. However, actually, 20 percent of the populace experiences psychological instability. I am in that 20 percent. There have been three particular occasions in my life where I haven't felt like me: The first occasion when it occurred, my grandmother had died, and I started encountering OCD indications around the age of 10. In those days, treatment wound up helping me break the cycle. Then, when I was in a second semester sophomore in school, and I fell into a winding of a sleeping disorder, tension, OCD, and sorrow brought about by awfulness. Family money related issues had an influence in my disturbance as well, and I had a feeling that I was losing the happy, quiet, rest adoring individual I had been. I had disassociated from myself, and all I needed to be was the individual before the injury.

Fortunately I went into treatment and (from the start hesitantly) began a stimulant. For around seven years, my manifestations were sensible. Then life struck by and by. A year ago, I was laid off; around a similar time, my uncle died. To state my body didn't respond well to the monetary weight and grief is putting it mildly. I created PTSD, my a sleeping disorder returned furiously, my OCD contemplations were steady, and my tension was deadening. I started to fear the things I once cherished: sprucing up, wearing cosmetics, going to shows, composing, and spending time with companions felt unbearable.

When you're sufficiently frantic, you'll successfully feel like you once more. For me, that implied taking a stab at something I had at no other time considered: hypnosis.

For individuals living with OCD, PTSD, fears, tension, or sadness, now and then treatment and prescription don't feel sufficiently like. That is the place hypnosis comes in. "Uneasiness is really self-hypnosis in a negative manner — when you [practice] hypnosis, you reinvent the brain with different convictions," trance inducer and psychotherapist Fayina Cohen says. She includes that the generalizations about hypnosis being phony or for hipsters are only that: generalizations.

Be that as it may, the shame and suspicion joined to hypnosis mean many individuals battling with psychological wellness issues don't have any acquaintance with it's a genuine alternative for them. My specialist, whom I credit with a huge amount of my enhancements, prescribed I attempt hypnosis. I, obviously, responded like a great many people: with genuine questions. I envisioned somebody waving a long, gold chain associated with a pocket watch over my face while I marvelously dropped. Be that as it may, when you're scarcely ready to work, you'll attempt pretty much anything. That is the manner by which I came to attempt hypnosis, and how I turned into an adherent to its capacity.

Meetings with my trance inducer started with talk treatment that assisted with illuminating the subsequent part, the hypnosis session itself. My subliminal specialist read from a painstakingly made content, which she balanced every week dependent on the issues we were focusing on. The sessions would run from 15 to 30 minutes, and for around eight months, I had schoolwork: to tune in to a chronicle before I would hit the sack.

The chronicles themselves don't generally bode well, yet implanted in them are directions focused at your intuitive personality. The directions are intended to bring you into an increasingly loosened up state – much the same as what you feel when you dream or when you miss a leave driving on the interstate (something many refer to as "parkway hypnosis"). "Your intuitive personality is stacked with pessimistic messages, so it's important to have a subliminal specialist get this stuff out for you," clarifies certified clinical trance specialist Joanne Ferdman of Theta Healing Arts in Huntington, New York. "Hypnotherapy is incredible for dealing with your considerations, getting out negative encounters and giving you enabling messages." But while your psyche is taking in said musings, hypnosis wouldn't fret control. "Hypnosis isn't something that can cause you to accomplish something without wanting to," clarifies Ferdman. "Your cognizant personality definitely comprehends what you need to take a shot at. I can't give you a recommendation that your cognizant personality isn't in finished concurrence with."

When it comes to results, timing is different for everybody. A few people see full changes — including more prominent unwinding, inspiration, and sentiment of control — in only a couple of sessions; others take more time to begin to mend. It relies upon the individual and the condition of their subliminal. As indicated by Ferdman, "We have 60,000 musings every day, and the greater part of them are negative." The greater cynicism you're managing, the more it might produce to see the results of hypnosis — regardless of the amount you intentionally need things to change.

Basically, hypnosis is a progression of suggestions to lessen uneasiness and dread, urging customers' psyches to go in increasingly positive ways when they feel overpowered by antagonism. In some cases it's fundamental for subliminal specialists to get out past encounters, which implies they'll accomplish something many refer to as "relapse" — they will manage you back to the first run through a horrendous encounter happened and assist you with handling it so you can discharge it from your intuitive.

If you're still with me, and charmed, you're not the only one. As indicated by subliminal specialists, hypnosis is turning into an all the more normally utilized practice. "Because of the Internet, more instruction removes the fantasy of hypnosis," Cohen says. "Over the most recent 10 years, I've been getting more calls about hypnosis than any other time in recent memory."

Here are a few things to remember if you're willing to check out hypnosis:

Discover a subliminal specialist you trust. Do your exploration, ask about their preparation and certification, and solicit to address past customers from theirs. Trust in your consideration supplier, whatever their claim to fame, is critical.

Concentrate on your inspiration to change. You may not be completely persuaded of the potential from the start, yet if you stay liberal and stick with it, results will probably follow.

Hypnosis is an association. Both you and your subliminal specialist cooperate in the recuperating procedure. Regardless of whether you're tuning in to your subliminal specialist read a content or taking in their tapes on rehash, it takes two.

You don't should be effectively tuning in for hypnosis to work. The directions and messages your subliminal specialist inserts in your content are consumed by the intuitive personality

You are in charge of your session. You despite everything have unrestrained choice, and you're not in a daze. The trance inducer is only there to encourage.

That is no joke "solid willed" to be spellbound. Your trance specialist is helping you to spellbind yourself – you're not surrendering or fooling yourself into a perspective you would prefer really not to enter. This is something you're accomplishing for you, as a feature of a full treatment plan you and your consideration suppliers turn out together.

At last, hypnosis wasn't a simple or programmed fix. It required persistence, responsibility, and consistency in appearing at my arrangements and tuning in to my chronicles. Be that as it may, I'm so happy I gave hypnosis a possibility. I consider it one of the restorative systems that helped me feel like myself again – and that has been worth consistently I've spent on it.

BE FREE FROM YOUR SUBCONSCIOUS MIND

Your mind is worked to fortify and manage your life.

Your subliminal personality has something many refer to as a homeostatic drive, which controls capacities like internal heat level, heartbeat and relaxing. Brian Tracy clarified it like this: "Through your autonomic sensory system, [your homeostatic impulse] keeps up a parity among the several synthetic substances in your billions of cells with the goal that your whole physical machine works in complete concordance more often than not."

In any case, what numerous individuals don't understand is that similarly as your mind is worked to direct your physical self, as does it attempt to manage your psychological self. Your brain is continually sifting and drawing out into the open data and boosts that avows your previous convictions (this is referred to in brain science as affirmation inclination) just as giving you rehashed contemplations and driving forces that copy and mirror what you've done before.

Your intuitive personality is the guardian of your usual range of familiarity.

It is likewise the domain where you can either habituate yourself to expect, and routinely look for the activities that would fabricate and strengthen, the best achievement, satisfaction, completeness or recuperating of your life.

Today In: Leadership

Here, a couple of approaches to begin retraining your psyche to be your partner, not your foe.

1. Be eager to see the unchangeable change.

Advanced

5 Myths About High School Interns (And Why You Should Hire Them)

The initial phase in making gigantic change in your life isn't really accepting that it's conceivable, it's being eager to check whether it is conceivable.

You won't have the option to bounce from being a finished doubter to a wholehearted adherent. The progression between those is simply being available to seeing what could be conceivable. You could perhaps have a go at sending a couple "terrifying messages," in which you suggestion a customer or accomplice for something that they don't have any motivation to react to. You may have two or three dozen overlooked messages, however in the long run, somebody will react.

The fact is that you're willing to check whether its conceivable... that is the thing that will transform you.

2. Give yourself authorization to be effective.

Rather than disgorging the regular old account of accepting you'll be glad once you're 10 pounds, one advancement and two life occasions down-the-line, take a shot at changing your internal monolog to: "I permit my life to be acceptable."
Give yourself authorization to be cheerful and effective, and not feel remorseful about it. If you have a subliminal relationship between progress being irreverent, or degenerate, obviously you're not going to do what you have to do to carry on with the life you need to live. Rather, give yourself consent to step into an entire, upbeat, healthy, grounded and important presence.
3. Try not to permit others' feelings of dread to cast shadows of uncertainty.
The manner in which individuals react to updates on your prosperity will disclose to you how they are truly getting along in their lives.

If you report your commitment, individuals who are in upbeat relationships will be cheerful for you. Individuals who are in miserable relationships will caution you that it is difficult and that you ought to make the most of your residual time as "single" people.
The fact of the matter is that others' feelings of dread are projections of their own circumstances. They don't have anything to do with what you are or aren't able to do.
4. Encircle yourself with uplifting feedback.

Keep a container of champagne in the ice chest. Change your morning caution on your telephone to peruse the message: "CONGRATULATIONS!!!" Make sure that the things that you see and contact frequently bring you energy and cheerfulness. Keep a helpful note on a post-it by your PC. Unfollow individuals who cause you to feel terrible about yourself and follow the individuals who are continually posting inspirational messages and intriguing thoughts. Make your newsfeed a spot that can catalyze your development, rather than decreasing your impression of your value.

5. Talk your prosperity as a present certainty, not a likely arrangement.

Despite the fact that you shouldn't make statements like "I drive a convertible," or "I am a CEO," if they are not in truth evident, do begin talking about what it is you deeply desire not in the setting that you will one day seek after it, yet that you are now living it.

Rather than saying: "I plan to do that one day," state, "I am strategizing how to do that now." Instead of reasoning: "I will be glad when I am in a different spot in my life," think, "I am totally equipped for being upbeat right here and at the present time, nothing is keeping me down."

6. Make a dream space.

Having the option to envision what it is you look for from your life is significant for making it, because if you don't have the foggiest idea where you're going, you won't know what direction to turn first.

When you have a perfectly clear picture in your psyche for what it is you need and how it is you need to live, you are then equipped for starting to sanction and make it. If you are as yet cloudy or torn between what you need, you will be rendered unequipped for taking genuine, important activity toward anything.

Regardless of whether you utilize a Pinterest board, blog, journal or board, set up words and pictures that speak to what you need and how you need to live.

7. Identify your obstruction.

When our subliminal personalities keep us away from seeking after something that we love, it is because we are holding a clashing conviction about it.

To identify your obstruction, question yourself. Wonder why you feel better when you linger, or why getting what you truly need could really place you in a spot that causes you to feel more defenseless than any time in recent memory. Figure out how to address those issues before you continue.

8. Have an all-inclusive strategy for your life.

Disregard five or even multi year plans; so much changes after some time it's about difficult to set objectives that you'll have the option to keep. No doubt, new or far better open doors will surface, and however your life won't appear as though you suspected it would, you're in an ideal situation for that.
Rather, have a ground breaking strategy. Identify your guiding principle and inspirations. Ask yourself what is a definitive objective of what you need to achieve while you are alive; envision the sort of inheritance you need to leave. When you have your Big Picture esteems identified, you can settle on choices for the long haul that line up with your actual self.

9. Start an appreciation diary.

The most ideal approach to begin placing yourself in a headspace of "having" instead of "needing" is to start an appreciation practice. By communicating a debt of gratitude is in order for all that you do have, you shift your mentality from being ravenous for change to feeling happy with where you are at. Nothing polarizes bounty to you like appreciation. There's a platitude that once you trust you have enough, you are available to getting to an ever increasing extent and then some. That is without a doubt genuine.

10. Begin requesting what you need, regardless of whether you realize you'll be denied.

If somebody requests that you do a counseling venture, request the measure of cash you genuinely need to gain for it. If you will probably get an advancement in your association, plunk down with your higher up and make your aims known. Contact brands you need to work with. Begin requesting what you need, regardless of whether you have no motivation to accept that anybody will really give you any of those things. In the long run, they will.

11. Discharge your connection to the "how."

Your main responsibility is to identify the what, and afterward to work couple with others for the how.

If you will likely work remotely and maintain your own business, rather than surrendering if your first endeavor falls flat, take a stab at reconsidering by what other means you could accomplish your definitive vision in another manner that is all the more monetarily worthwhile.

The fact is that life will consistently astonish you with how things work out as expected. Rather than being fanatically appended to each and every detail working out the manner in which you figure it should, be available to potential and probability, regardless of whether it's something you never envisioned.

12. Encircle yourself with partners.

Begin investing energy with individuals who are aggressive, steady and inventive.

If you're hanging out each end of the week with individuals who are in like manner as discontent with their lives, you won't get a wealth of help if you attempt to break free and do your own thing. Recall that you will really become who you invest the most energy with, and pick who that is cautiously.

13. Fill your "dead air" time with insistence and inspiration.

When you're on your drive every morning, tune in to an inspirational discourse or digital recording. While you're doing the dishes or driving, tune into a television show that identifies with the sort of business you're attempting to do. Imbue your life with however much assertion and inspiration as could reasonably be expected. You may need to hear the exercises more than once, yet they will saturate your cerebrum after some time, and in the end, you will wind up following up on insight got from the individuals who are the place you need to be.

Intuitive Mind Power

The intensity of your intuitive personality goes farther than you may might suspect.

No play on words proposed.

I'm certain you'll concur with me when I state our cerebrums are very confused.

In any case, you may be amazed by how much control we have over its programming.

Before I find a good pace:

Allows first pause for a minute to consider the way that your intuitive personality resembles an immense memory bank. Its ability is for all intents and purposes boundless and it for all time stores everything that ever transpires

When you arrive at the age of 21, you've as of now forever put away more than one hundred times the substance of the whole Encyclopedia Britannica.

Under hypnosis, more established individuals can often recollect, with flawless lucidity, occasions from fifty years prior. Your oblivious memory is for all intents and purposes great. It is your cognizant review that is suspect.

The capacity of your subliminal personality is to store and recover information. Its main responsibility is to guarantee that you react precisely the manner in which you are customized. Your intuitive personality makes all that you state and do fit an example steady with your self-idea, your "lord program." This is the reason rehashing constructive insistences are so compelling — you can really reconstruct your own idea designs by slipping in constructive and achievement situated sound chomps.

This is the reason persuasive exercises, for example, perusing helpful statements, are so effective for individuals focused on positive reasoning. By concentrating your contemplations on uplifting thoughts, your intuitive will start to actualize a positive example from your perspective and your point of view.

Your intuitive personality is abstract. It doesn't think or reason freely; it only complies with the directions it gets from your cognizant personality. Similarly as your cognizant personality can be thought of as the plant specialist, planting seeds, your intuitive personality can be thought of as the nursery, or ripe soil, in which the seeds develop and develop. This is another motivation behind why bridling the intensity of positive reasoning is critical to the establishment of your whole perspective.

Your cognizant personality directions and your intuitive personality complies.

Your intuitive personality is an unquestioning worker that works day and night to make your conduct fits an example steady with your emotionalized contemplations, expectations, and wants. Your intuitive personality develops either blossoms or weeds in the nursery of your life, whichever you plant by the psychological counterparts you make.

Your intuitive personality has what is known as a homeostatic motivation. It keeps your internal heat level at 98.6 degrees Fahrenheit, similarly as it keeps you breathing normally and keeps your heart pulsating at a specific rate. Through your autonomic sensory system, it keeps up an equalization among the many synthetic substances in your billions of cells with the goal that your whole physical machine works in complete concordance more often than not.

Your subliminal personality additionally rehearses homeostasis in your psychological domain, by keeping you thinking and acting in a way steady with what you have done and said before.

Every one of your propensities for speculation and acting are put away in your intuitive personality. It has retained all your customary ranges of familiarity and it attempts to keep you in them. This is the reason it's so imperative to make composing SMART objectives a customary propensity. After time, remaining profitable and concentrating on the entirety of your objectives will turn out to be a piece of your customary range of familiarity.

Your intuitive personality makes you feel sincerely and genuinely awkward whenever you endeavor to do anything new or different or to change any of your set up examples of conduct. The feeling of dread and distress are mental signs that your intuitive has been actuated. However, it's been attempting to build up those personal conduct standards out of sight some time before you'll ever notice such sentiments.

The inclination to focus on these examples is one motivation behind why propensities can be so difficult to break. In any case, when you figure out how to deliberately make such examples, you can tackle the intensity of propensity and intentionally impart new safe places to which your subliminal will adjust.

You can feel your subliminal pulling you back toward your usual range of familiarity each time you take a stab at something new. In any event, contemplating accomplishing something other than what's expected based on what you're acclimated with will cause you to feel tense and uncomfortable.

This is the reason time the executives tips might be harder to actualize from the start, yet once they become propensity or routine they will remain in your usual range of familiarity. In doing as such, you've reinvented your intuitive to work in support of you.

Predominant people are continually extending themselves, propelling themselves out of their customary ranges of familiarity. They are mindful how rapidly the safe place, in any zone, turns into a trench. They realize that lack of concern is the incredible foe of imagination and future conceivable outcomes.

For you to develop, to escape your customary range of familiarity, you must be happy to feel ungainly and awkward doing new things the initial barely any occasions. If it merits progressing admirably, it merits doing ineffectively until you figure out it, until you build up another safe place at another, more elevated level of fitness.

For those hoping to grow their domain of safe places, I energetically suggest considering the propensities for effective individuals as they are the examples ordinarily received by the psyches of extraordinary pioneers and masterminds. Opening the intensity of these practices will put you one bit nearer to having the option to cause very similar things to occur in your life.

Learning systems to reconstruct your subliminal personality will assist you with trusting in yourself because your certainty will never again be tested by dread of the obscure. In any case, more significantly, doing so will prepare your mind to be in accordance with your actual wants, dreams, and life objectives. The more on top of your intuitive you become, the closer you will be to getting through to progress. For instance, you may have a thought for a book that has been on your back burner for quite a long time. With the correct degree of certainty, you'll make the following stride in figuring out how to compose a book, as opposed to sticking to the fantasy, however never acting.

Keep in mind:

Making prompt move on your thoughts is an amazing key to progress. Liberating yourself from self-constraining convictions – or questions – is the initial step to being prepared for activity.

INSTRUCTIONS TO REPROGRAM YOUR SUBCONSCIOUS MIND

"Whatever we plant in our intuitive personality and support with redundancy and feeling will one day become a reality" — Earl Nightingale

Your intuitive personality has tremendous force in controlling your life encounters — from the kinds of nourishment you eat to the moves you make every day, the degree of pay you procure, and even how you respond to unpleasant circumstances.

All of it is guided by your subliminal convictions and translations.

To put it plainly, your subliminal personality resembles the auto-pilot highlight on a plane. It has been pre-modified to follow a specific course and you can't veer off from that course except if you change the headings customized into it first.

What Is The Subconscious Mind?

"plasma ball computerized backdrop" by Josh Riemer on Unsplash

The "intuitive" is the piece of your mind that works underneath your typical degree of waking awareness.

At this moment you're essentially utilizing your cognizant personality to peruse these words and assimilate their importance, yet underneath that psychological center, your intuitive personality is hectically working off camera, engrossing or dismissing data dependent on a current discernment you have of your general surroundings.

This current observation started shaping when you were a newborn child.

With each experience, your subliminal personality absorbs data like a wipe.

It dismissed nothing while you were youthful because you didn't have any prior convictions to repudiate what it saw. It basically acknowledged that the entirety of the data you got during your initial youth was valid.

You can most likely observe why this turns into an issue sometime down the road. Each time somebody called you inept, useless, slow, apathetic, or more regrettable, your subliminal personality just put away the data away for reference.

You may likewise have gotten messages about your potential in life or confinements you'll confront dependent on your physical capacities, skin shading, sexual orientation, or monetary status.

When you were 7 or 8 years of age, you previously had a strong establishment of conviction dependent on such programming from individuals in your life, network shows you viewed, and other natural influences.

How Does This 'Old' Programming Affect You Now?

"programming language codes" by Markus Spiske on Unsplash

Presently that you're a grown-up, you may feel that you can basically dispose of the harmful or false messages you consumed during your initial life,

however, it's not exactly that basic.

Recall that the entirety of this data is put away beneath your degree of cognizant mindfulness. The main time you become mindful of it is when it confines your advancement in making a decent, fruitful and profitable life.

Have you at any point attempted to accomplish an objective and continued subverting yourself every step of the way? Enraging, right? Know that you're not flawed or bound to bomb regardless of what you do.

Almost certain you are very brave modified messages that conflict with the new conditions you need to make.

This is fantastic news because it implies,

you can accomplish pretty much anything if you first set aside the effort to reconstruct your intuitive personality!

The Programming Is Still Going On

"string light representation photography of lady wearing eyeglasses" by YIFEI CHEN on Unsplash

Before we find how to reconstruct your psyche, it's critical to realize that,
the programming despite everything proceeds right up 'til the present time.
With each experience you have, you make certain inferences and store the messages that will manage your future activities.
For instance, what sort of message do you think would be put away if you were dismissed by somebody you thought about?
Your subliminal personality — that smart analyst — would promptly go chasing through your recollections and find different instances of dismissal — like that time your closest companion dumped you to spend time with the more well known children — and make a determination that you're by one way or another disgraceful or unlovable and have the right to be dismissed.
Presently, here's the intriguing thing,
if you have an encounter that conflicts with a previously settled conviction, your subliminal personality will either dismiss it or reframe it so it obliges your current perspective on the real world.
Here's a model,
suppose you have a hidden conviction that you're ugly, and an alluring individual communicates an enthusiasm for finding a workable pace better.

Doubtlessly the first thing you're going to believe is that it must be a joke or a remorseless stunt. You will have a hard time believing that this individual could find you alluring because you as of now accept that you're ugly.

Underneath the outside of your cognizant mindfulness, your intuitive personality is shouting, "No chance! This individual is too alluring to possibly be keen on me, something isn't directly here... "

Then you'll either dismiss that individual before they can dismiss you, or in any case plan something for damage what could have been an extraordinary relationship.

Something very similar happens when you battle to accomplish your objectives. In the end you begin to accept that you aren't fit for progress, so you arrive at expect disappointment and wind up doing only that again and again.

You can most likely envision numerous different circumstances where your subliminal personality restrains you, yet reinventing it is a basic issue if you know how.

Step by step instructions to Reprogram Your Subconscious Mind

Photograph by Armand Khoury on Unsplash

There are a wide range of approaches to overwrite the constraining or harming messages that are put away in your subliminal personality.

You could work all the while with these techniques, however it'll be considerably more successful if you pick only a couple of strategies to begin. You need to give them your complete consideration as opposed to skipping around and weakening your endeavors.

Keep in mind, you can generally join extra methods after some time.

Ecological Influences

"sunflower field" by Gustavo Quepón on Unsplash

Have you at any point thought about the impact of your condition on your subliminal personality?

Recollect that your subliminal personality is retaining data continually and reaching inferences and shaping convictions dependent on that data.

If your day by day condition is filled with antagonism and strife, envision what sorts of messages are being consumed into your brain.

Your first activity is as far as possible the antagonism you're presented to from this minute on.

Abstain from viewing the news except if you totally should, and abstain from investing an excessive amount of energy with 'lethal' individuals.

Rather, search out constructive data to peruse and watch, and invest the vast majority of your energy with constructive, fruitful individuals.

After some time you'll find that all the more reassuring messages are being consumed into your brain, which will change the manner in which you see yourself and your latent capacity.

Representation

Your intuitive personality reacts well to pictures.

Perception is an incredible method to program your brain with positive, enabling pictures.

Take a stab at going through 10–15 minutes daily picturing positive scenes that component you and your life encounters.

Here are a few things you might need to picture:

Fulfilling connections

Energetic work

A beautiful home

Extraordinary get-aways

Whatever else you wish to bring into your life

As you do this reliably, you wind up redrawing the negative pictures put away from your past encounters, fears, stresses, and questions.

To help the intensity of perception considerably further, make certain to radiate solid, positive feelings while you picture these magnificent things in your brain.

Permit sentiments of adoration, satisfaction, appreciation, and harmony to flow through you as though you were really having these encounters.

Your intuitive personality will assimilate the messages as though they're genuine!

This is the genuine excellence of perception – the ability to sidestep restricting messages and spotlight on satisfying pictures, which are all being retained directly into your subliminal to be replayed later.

Attestations

"difficult streets lead to beautiful goals work area stylistic theme" by Hello I'm Nik on Unsplash

Attestations are another compelling method to introduce positive messages into your intuitive.

They work best if you adhere to a couple of basic principles:

Word them emphatically, in the current state. State "I am confident and fruitful" as opposed to "I will be confident and effective" because concentrating on a future condition doesn't register with your subliminal personality – it knows just this minute. Additionally, utilize positive explanations. Saying "I am not a disappointment" is figured as "I am a disappointment" since your intuitive can't process negatives.

Call up the comparing sentiments. Saying "I am well off" while feeling poor just sends conflicting messages to your subliminal. Whatever words you're stating at that point, endeavor to feel the relating feelings because your subliminal will be increasingly able to trust it.

Rehash, rehash, rehash. Confirmations don't work if you state them just a few times. Recount them commonly for the duration of the day for the best outcomes. The beneficial thing about this is you can say attestations to yourself, so they can fit flawlessly into your daily schedule.

Mind Entrainment Binaural Beats

"silver earphones over dark surface" by Frank Septillion on Unsplash

Another well known technique is the utilization of sound accounts that intentionally modify the recurrence of your brainwaves.

It might seem like something out of a science fiction motion picture, however reports from individuals who've attempted these sound projects are overwhelmingly positive.

Your brainwaves fall into a specific recurrence relying upon what you're doing at some random time:

Gamma when you're occupied with certain engine capacities

Beta when you're completely cognizant and effectively focusing

Alpha when you're loose

Theta when you're tired or softly resting

Delta when you're in profound rest

"Binaural beats" result when two tones are played at differing frequencies, setting off your brainwaves to follow a different example.

For instance, if you needed to shift from worried to loosened up you would tune in to a sound that triggers the alpha state.
These sound projects can help you reconstruct your subliminal personality by, making an increasingly open gathering for introducing positive messages.
Research has indicated that your intuitive personality is progressively open to new data when you're loose, for example, in the alpha or theta states.
Utilizing cerebrum entrainment sound projects alongside insistences or representation can be an amazing mix, because your subliminal personality lets down its guards so it can without much of a stretch ingest any message you wish to program in.
Essentially unwind and center around positive pictures!
Hypnosis
"lady lying on green grasses" by Jacob Townsend on Unsplash
Hypnosis can be compelling similarly as mind entrainment programs, aside from without the utilization of brainwave-changing frequencies.
Rather, the trance inducer step by step talks you into an increasingly loose and open state and conveys enabling, positive messages to your subliminal personality.

Self-hypnosis is another well-known choice — you essentially use pre-recorded sound projects rather than a live hypnosis session. You can even record your own self-hypnosis CDs so you'll hear your own voice discussing positive insistences while you're in a casual state.

The most effective method to Know If Your Reprogramming Efforts Are Working

"lady riding on back of man" via Carly Rae Hobbins on Unsplash

One of the most testing parts of reconstructing your intuitive personality is that you can't look inside and see what's still there that may should be changed.

Rather, you'll need to build up a solid feeling of mindfulness so you can get self-disrupting conduct before it escapes hand.

All things being equal, there are still some away from of progress that you may perceive:

You start feeling more grounded, more confident and more joyful.

You find yourself additionally ready to face challenges and face difficulties.

Your fantasies and objectives don't appear to be overpowering any longer — simply energizing.

You feel a more profound feeling of internal harmony, as though inward conflicts are dissolving.

You draw in more chances to extend and develop in each aspect of your life.

To put it plainly, you'll realize when changes are occurring in your subliminal personality because you'll see a shift in both your inward and external being.

The proof is typically unquestionable!

Steady, Persistent Reinforcement

"lady sitting on cover situated on shoreline" by Cody Black on Unsplash

It's essential to give this reconstructing procedure time to work.

Try not to hope to see quick changes — every so often that can occur, however more often it requires some investment.

Be exceptionally steady and relentless with the strategies you decide to introduce progressively positive messages into your subliminal personality.

When these changes become clear, you'll feel roused to continue pushing ahead,

in any case, until that occurs,

stay with it and realize that these progressions are lifelong, amazing, and well worth hanging tight for!

METHODOLOGIES TO STOP OVERTHINKING AND START GOAL-SETTING

What do Oprah Winfrey and Mark Cuban share for all intents and purpose? Besides being enormously fruitful news big shots (also, tycoons), they didn't let early-profession difficulties obstruct their streets to progress.

Informed that she didn't have the hacks for TV news, Winfrey was terminated from her first correspondent gig. Cuban was chopped out from a vocation as a product sales rep in the wake of ignoring his manager so as to make a beneficial deal. Significant side note - he never worked for any other person again. Both Winfrey and Cuban proceeded to assemble their own realms.

Strength is a basic attribute for prevailing as a business person. Rumination, then again - harping on negative considerations and misfortunes - can wreck you from accomplishing your objectives. That is because ruminating disrupts certain key aptitudes for maintaining your own business.

Fortunately, with some mindfulness and practice, it's conceivable to bring an end to your propensity for ruminating. Above all, a more critical take a gander at the impacts of getting trapped in negative idea circles.

What's the damage of rumination?

First off, ruminating harms your capacity to think plainly and tackle issues. As indicated by look into by late Yale University analyst Susan Nolen-Hoeksema, ruminators battle to discover answers for theoretical issues, conceivably because of their negative viewpoints.

In any event, when they do think of arrangements, ruminators are either moderate or unfit to institute them. Said Nolen-Hoeksema, "the rumination itself may instigate a degree of vulnerability and immobilization that makes it difficult for them to push ahead." For instance, an examination by analysts at UC Riverside indicated that ladies who will in general ruminate assumed control over a month longer to look for medicinal consideration in the wake of finding a bosom protuberance.

Any originator will let you know - propelling a business is tied in with tackling an issue, and it doesn't need to be noteworthy.

Thirteen years prior I figured the world could utilize a superior, more easy to use online structure developer, so I established JotForm. I didn't decide to rehash an already solved problem, however to unravel an issue I experienced consistently while working for different organizations. Today, JotForm helps 4.5 million clients who were are having a similar basic issue that I was.

Then, there are the everyday issues that authors face - with clients, representatives, accomplices and business when all is said in done. In the present economy, where plans of action should continually develop, unwavering discernment and critical thinking is basic.

In her examination, Nolen-Hoeksema likewise found that ruminators will in general drive away social help and that the two of them request and get less assistance.

Being a business visionary may seem like a performance adventure, yet in actuality, you can't grow a business without help. It's particularly significant for beginning period organizers, who face late evenings, high pressure and oftentimes feel separated from loved ones.

Indeed, even at my stage, over 10 years into the game, I perceive the proceeding with estimation of help. I connect when I know another person in my group is better qualified to deal with an assignment, when I need target input on an item thought or when I have to calibrate a system.

Over everything, the pressure related with constant negative reasoning can prompt a large group of health issues - from stifled invulnerable working to expanded danger of coronary issues.

Because ruminating adversely influences key parts of a business person's activity and prosperity, it merits making sense of how to check contrary idea circles from the beginning.

Four stages to quit ruminating and start objective setting.

1. Recognize negative reasoning.

Breaking destructive idea cycles starts with mindfulness. Except if you recognize that you're ruminating, you'll always be unable to shorten it. Furthermore, burning through so much mental effort in your inside world renders you less proactive in the outside.

"The more we are occupied with overthinking, the less [we're] really getting things done in the physical condition," clarifies clinical clinician David Carbonell Everybody overthinks once in a while, yet if you wind up fixating on a negative thought or experience, make a stride back and focus on what's going on in your mind. Be an eyewitness for a second. Attempt to identify the substance of your negative contemplations. Then, you can deal with tending to them.

2. Switch into critical thinking mode and have an objective setting session.

Oftentimes, we ruminate on things outside of our present control. That is the reason it's essential to consider whether you can do anything right presently to determine what you're ruminating about.

If you can, make a rundown of steps to move in the direction of enhancing the circumstance. State, for instance, I made a disaster during an introduction. My rundown would include: email participants a clarification email, plan additional opportunity to get ready for my next introduction, and so on. Objective setting is vital.

Or then again, if you can't manage the issue currently, set an opportunity to concentrate on it later. "Odds are it won't trouble you particularly when you get together with it - and you will have the option to make the most of your life during the remainder of the day," composes Robert Leahy, Director of the American Institute for Cognitive Therapy.

3. Start to perspire.

Because nothing settles an overactive personality like some pressure diminishing endorphins, practice is perhaps the best tale for ruminating. When you work out, you're additionally increasingly occupied with your present movement - i.e., progressively careful, which departs mental less space to ruminate.

Regardless of whether it's biking, running, boxing or yoga - do whichever type of activity you appreciate. Indeed, even an energetic stroll during your lunch break can help clear the head. Or on the other hand, contingent upon the length of your drive, you can stroll to work like Jack Dorsey. The Twitter and Square CEO has said that going for an opportunity to stroll the five miles to work each day is the most beneficial venture he's at any point made.

In his words: "It's a very clearing time. I need to put as a lot of startling potential before me because I figure something that you don't plan will consistently make you think differently."

4. Treat yourself to some compassion.

Oftentimes, we're harsher on ourselves than we are with others. For instance, if a partner had an introduction blip, you likely wouldn't denounce them as a horrible speaker. You'd probably think they were simply having an off-day.

Put forth an attempt to be objective. Consider the guidance you'd provide for a companion or adored one in your circumstance, then attempt to take that equivalent compassionate tone with yourself. If your ruminating proceeds, envision how you'll feel in half a month from now. That is the means by which you'll feel soon enough.

Also, recall, even the best individuals endure periodic difficulties. What characterizes them isn't letting those difficulties lose them track.

Individuals come up with a wide range of reasons for why they're not coming to their however the basic truth is this: if you're not achieving what you need in life, it's presumably because you're not being strategic in seeking after your objectives.

The uplifting news? A large number of the basic reasons why you're not arriving at your objectives are handily cured. Truly! Right now, address some regular things that keep individuals away from arriving at their objectives and offer proposals for how you can methodicallly expel the barricades that are shielding you from pushing ahead.

An absence of specific objectives.

You will never arrive at your objectives if you don't have specific objectives spread out in the first place.

If your objectives are unclear, as "get rich" or "be effective", that is about as accommodating as attempting to find a workable pace address in Miami by entering "Florida" in your GPS. It may get you some place in the locale of your objective, yet not rapidly or proficiently.

To accomplish your objectives, the initial step is truly getting firm on what your objectives really are. For instance, rather than an objective of "purchase a house," consider defining an objective like "spare $50,000 in the following two years so I can place an up front installment on a house in X neighborhood."

With a specific objective to move in the direction of you can make an arrangement with specific achievements to arrive.

A daily schedule.

You may discover schedules exhausting, yet they convey results. Consider, for example, that probably the best individuals have a customary schedule that starts with getting up right on time. They utilize this opportunity to get everyday assignments off the beaten path and by and large get intellectually arranged for the day ahead. Their morning is organized so they can move toward the workday with lucidity and center, and not be pulled in such a large number of headings.

If you're simply taking a blind leap of faith consistently, your vocation results will be also sporadic. To accomplish specific objectives, set a standard that will permit you to accomplish achievements without packing. Work gradually yet relentlessly toward them.

Direction.

Similarly as a GPS can help get you to the goal quicker and simpler than utilizing an old school guide and exploring the streets yourself, appropriate direction can assist you with arriving at your objectives.

If you don't have confidence in the intensity of a coach, think about this: Mark Zuckerberg, Oprah, and Bill Gates all acknowledge their guides for helping them discover the achievement that they proceeded to accomplish. By getting yourself a guide, you're giving yourself a sort of quick forward catch on your vocation. From a tutor, you can pick up direction, heading, guidance, thus considerably more. Need to become fruitful sooner? Get a guide.

Responsibility.

To jump on track is one thing...but to remain on track is another. What balanced governance do you have set up to keep yourself responsible?

Indeed, even the most optimistic individuals experience difficulty remaining propelled some of the time. A responsibility accomplice can help. This is somebody who does customary registration with you to perceive how you're advancing toward your objectives. A decent responsibility accomplice can be just about anybody - a collaborator, a companion or a relative. It simply should be somebody who can dependably check in with you about how you are getting along on arriving at your objectives to assist you with remaining responsible.

Not gaining from your slip-ups.

Seeking after grand objectives resembles ascending a major tall mountain: regardless, will undoubtedly lurch two or multiple times en route. While you ought to effectively attempt to keep away from botches, you ought to recognize that a couple of will most likely happen en route.

Instead of letting botches squash you, attempt to gain from them. As a silver coating, what feels obliterating at one point may spare you from an a lot greater error later if you're ready to gain proficiency with your exercise the first run through!

NEED TO BE SUCCESSFUL? STOP OVERTHINKING.

What hath been, it is what will be; and that which is done is what will be done: and there is no new thing under the sun." – When you've been around as long as I have, you can think back over your life and note the occasions that changed your point of view and affected how things showed up for you. They're called defining moments. They're rare, and in light of current circumstances. Such a large number of and your life would be one major disordered chaos.

Of perhaps five or six significant defining moments that really impacted the result for me, one stands separated. Furthermore, I'm going to impart it to you because it could possibly have a genuine effect for you, as it accomplished for me.

I'm not actually a book of scriptures researcher, yet I do feel weak at the knees over the straightforward graceful intelligence of the Book of Ecclesiastes. I really have my own renditions of a portion of its key messages that I present every once in a while, including this one: The more you live and the more shrewd you become, the more you'll understand how little you know ... and how little it is important.

Truly, I do acknowledge I'm no writer. It would not benefit from outside intervention.

Anyway, I was acquainted with Ecclesiastes when I expected to become familiar with a significant exercise – that all the information and accomplishments on the planet don't mean beans if you can't appreciate or if nothing else experience the valuable minutes that you're here. Before sufficiently long, it will all be finished, and you don't find a workable pace with you.

My concern was that I'd spent a decent piece of my life diverted by questions like, Why am I here? furthermore, What's my motivation in life? The day I chose to quit looking for answers and essentially experience life was a major defining moment. Amusingly, that was when the appropriate responses came. When I quit overthinking and concentrated essentially doing and being.

Like me, I see a significant number of you investing God realizes what amount of energy scanning for answers to diverting inquiries like, How to be fruitful? How to be cheerful? How to be rich? How to be well known? How to be increasingly gainful? How to be less restless? How to be [fill in the blank]?

Listen to this. Sometime in the not so distant future, you might just glance back at your life and acknowledge you've discovered the appropriate responses you looked for, yet like me, you'll likewise understand that you didn't discover them by posing a great deal of inquiries. I realize that seems like an oddity, so let me clarify.

Actually, life is essential. You're brought into the world with endurance impulses. You learn experimentation at an early age (strolling and such). In school they show you how to reason (ideally). From that point you go out and experience and settle on decisions. You gain certainty from great ones, and take in exercises from terrible ones. Do this process again.

That little preview of life uncovers the four key components that issue most in deciding how things show up for you: Instincts, smarts, understanding, and decisions. Obviously there are different components: attributes, abilities, aptitudes, conduct, and karma, to give some examples.

Be that as it may, this is what everybody appears to experience difficulty understanding, nowadays. "Cheerful," "effective," "rich," and "well known" are on the whole results that are dictated by the various variables I just discussed. If you need to accomplish positive results, you'd be astute to heed your gut feelings, think sensibly, gain understanding, and use sound judgment.

What's more, trust me when I let you know, there are no alternate routes to the result. The sooner you understand that and quit scanning for them – the sooner you quit overthinking and center essentially around doing and being – the sooner you'll accomplish the result you're searching for.

I wager I realize what some of you are thinking. You hear what I'm stating, however you believe It's different at this point. What with web based life, the blogosphere, self improvement guides, courses, and all that, I wager you think the appropriate responses are out there. All things considered, I'm here to disclose to you that they're most certainly not.

Things being what they are, don't simply believe me. Here's a little insight, civility of Ecclesiastes 1:9, "what hath been, it is what will be; and that which is done is what will be done: and there is no new thing under the sun."

It implies that things are not different at this point. They're equivalent to they've generally been. It would be lamentable if some of you spent your whole lives without acknowledging how obvious that is. Everything I can say is, I'm happy I discovered that exercise sooner, instead of later.

We as a whole have objectives in life. Every single one of us needs to accomplish something, regardless of whether incredible or little, sooner or later in our lives. We have profound situated expectations and dreams for the future and a deep yearning to achieve some extraordinary accomplishments. It's sewed into the very texture of our general public, woven into the center of what our identity is, where it counts inside. It's embellished in our DNA, hereditarily pre-dispositioned, for minor endurance, yet in addition with a longing enthusiasm to flourish.

Truth be told, it's a piece of what's made us as a culture into who we seem to be. Our species has something other than endure; we've truly flourished, accomplishing stunning outcomes because of the wild-looked at developments that have started the likelihood to make the apparently inconceivable a reality in our lives. Have we wanted for the moon, however we've likewise gone for the stars.

Plainly, we've accomplished some huge objectives in life. Over the planet, we've achieved what was once thought to live just in the domain of human creative mind, or simply the subject of sci-fi dream. However, while our general public and culture appear to make galactic jumps forward and accomplishing shocking objectives, as people, we think that its harder to see things through when it goes to our own objectives.

It is difficult accomplishing your objectives in life. That much is sure. In any case, couple that with our voracious hunger for moment gratification and our proclivity to run on the apparently unending libertine treadmill - where we're continually going after an option that is superior to anything we have today - it's no big surprise that we get disappointed while attempting to accomplish extraordinary things. When disappointment reappears and we endure the disparagement of open embarrassment, it's no big surprise why we discover it so difficult to accomplish our objectives in life.

However, there is a more straightforward way. The best issue that a great many people face is that they neglect to set their objectives the correct way. Also, when they do set their objectives, their methodology is all off-base. The most ideal approach to accomplish any objective in life is to set them the correct way, yet in addition to design and execute their activities as per accomplishing those fantasies after some time.

New Year's disorder.

A great many people partner the defining of their objectives with one day specifically - New Year's Eve. It's a period for a new beginning. A possibility for a fresh start. Be that as it may, the individuals who set objectives on New Year's Eve don't ordinarily oversee them. Truth be told, as indicated by one investigation by the University of Scranton, just eight percent of objectives set on New Year's Eve are really accomplished.

That is a 92 percent disappointment rate, which is quite sickening and unsettling when you consider it. But on the other hand that is because a great many people who set objectives on New Year's don't set them the correct way. You can't hope to accomplish your objectives when you turn out badly. This negates any formula for objective setting achievement that is out there.

Why would that be? Because defining objectives on New Year's Eve, or some other day so far as that is concerned, isn't possible discretionarily in the psyche. The objectives can't stay in theory. They must be emerged and characterized with a high level of specificity. Furthermore, they should be arranged and followed up on in the correct manner.

That may be the reason 34 percent of individuals abandon their New Year's objectives after the primary month. Following a half year, 54 percent have tumbled off track and surrendered. The chances are piled facing us because we're not defining objectives the correct way. When you follow a demonstrated arrangement for defining and accomplishing your objectives the correct way, you're bound to oversee things.

The 7 stages for accomplishing any objective.

Without a doubt, accomplishing any objective requires intense self-control. It includes a cognizant familiarity with our activities and the capacity to beat a portion of the unfortunate propensities that may be keeping us down. Imparting self-restraint into our lives is no simple errand. It requires an enduring regard for our activities and an unwavering drive for needing to accomplish something important.

In any case, moving past that, there's a demonstrated framework for accomplishing any objective. It includes seven separate advances and a framework called SMARTER objective setting. More intelligent objectives, an abbreviation, will permit you to accomplish about anything your heart wants. It permits you to breakdown the procedure into unmistakable advances, doing somewhat every day towards the accomplishment you had always wanted.

1 (S) - Get (S)pecific about your objectives

The initial phase in the SMARTER technique for objective setting is to get profoundly specific about what you expect to accomplish. You need to guarantee that it's quantifiable so it very well may be followed, yet you likewise need to place a lot of detail into what it is you plan to accomplish. You can't simply say you need to be rich. It doesn't work that way.

If you have cash objectives, they have to include a specific measure of cash. For instance, you expect to have a one million dollar total assets in the following two years, you intend to win $20,000 every month in the following a year by working up an assistance business, or whatever else so far as that is concerned. Yet, you should be intensely specific about it.

When you get specific about an objective, it appears. It moves from the theoretical into the real world. To do that, it must be recorded. It must move from your psyche to a bit of paper or a screen. What would you like to accomplish? What does your life resemble by then when you arrive at that objective? Who are your companions? What are you doing during the day? What propensities do you have? What time would you say you are awakening?

You truly need to depict the objective and your life in a lot of detail. If you intend to shed 50 pounds in the following a year, depict what your day resembles when you arrive at that objective. What's your abdomen size? What sorts of garments would you say you are wearing? What time would you say you are awakening to work out? What sorts of nourishments would you say you are eating or maintaining a strategic distance from? The more specific you get, the better.

2 (M) - Ensure that your objectives are (M)eaningful

Objectives can't simply be specific. The second step for accomplishing your objectives is to guarantee that they're significant. We will consistently accomplish more to accomplish an objective that has a profound attached importance to us than we will to accomplish something that is shallow. Along these lines, if you need to have a million dollar total assets because of the status it manages, you can disregard your odds for progress.

Rather, if you have cash objectives, and you partner a profound enough importance to them, then they're bound to be accomplished. You can't simply need things for needing them. You can't simply need to get in shape or get more cash-flow because those are objectives you've constantly needed. Why have you constantly needed them?

We will consistently accomplish more to accomplish things that are profoundly important to us. When those implications include things like family, opportunity, security, nation and love, we'll make a special effort to oversee things. We won't toss in that famous towel and surrender after we hit a couple hindrances or bomb over and over.

Bring a minute to record the implying that you're partner with your objectives. Burrow profound. It must be a significant importance. It must be something that you're willing to sacrifice everything for. Record this on a bit of paper or a screen. This is one of the most significant strides simultaneously.

3 (A) - Pick objectives that are (A)chievable.

I'm totally supportive of picking grandiose long haul objectives. Ten years not far off, we can accomplish anything as long as we buckle down during that whole period. However, when it goes to your one, two and even three-year objectives, guarantee that they're feasible. Try not to say that you're going to make a billion dollars in a year if you're at present vigorously under water.

When you pick objectives that are attainable, in addition to the fact that you are bound to accomplish them, however you can likewise build up some force all the while. It's energizing to achieve an objective that is at present distant, regardless of what that objective is. When you arrive, you're powered by the energy and excitement of arriving at your objective.

Discover objectives that are enormous, yet not difficult to accomplish, at any rate for your shorter-term objectives. Plan your year objectives with the goal that they go about as achievements or markers towards the more extended term, a lot greater objectives. Then, make certain to make a gigantic activity plan that will assist you with overseeing things.

4 (R) - The objectives must be (R)elevant.

How important are the objectives that you've chosen for your life and your future? It is safe to say that they are lined up with what your identity is? Do they resound with your guiding principle and convictions? Or then again, do they go in opposition to everything that you have confidence in? When we pick objectives that contradict some common norms of what our identity is, we think that its significantly more difficult to finish.

So how would you pick significant objectives for your life? One route is to bring a minute to write down everything that you esteem and have faith in. For instance, if you esteem trustworthiness, yet you feel that every single rich individuals are warped and some way or another arrived in such a state through some stealthy or wicked techniques, you may think that its difficult to accomplish enormous cash objectives.

What we trust in are likewise the result of things we've heard while growing up. Things like "cash doesn't fall from the sky," or "more cash, more issues," and "all men cheat and lie, etc, become instilled in our psyches, affecting all our considerations, feeling and resultant conduct.

Set aside the effort to write down the things that make you into what your identity is. Then, pick pertinent objectives that are in concordance with what you put stock in and esteem. You'll see your objective setting venture as considerably more amicable and liquid when you pick significant objectives to your life and who you are where it counts inside.

5 (T) - Make sure the objectives are (T)ime-bound.

Objectives must be time-bound so as to be feasible. When do you plan on accomplishing this objective? Don't simply say you need to get wealthy later on or make a million dollars in the following not many years. You need to pick a date on the schedule if you're not kidding about accomplishing that objective.

THE STYLES OF DECISION MAKING WHEN YOU USE HYPNOSIS TO QUIT OVERTHINKING

Viable and productive basic leadership is at the center of any business person's prosperity.

I had the joy of plunking down with Jeffrey Shinabarger, creator of Yes or No: How Your Everyday Decisions Will Forever Change Your Life and originator of Plywood People, a not-for-profit in Atlanta that "drives a network of new companies doing great."

Through his work with Plywood People, Shinabarger has instituted seven basic leadership styles subsequent to working with many individuals in "snapshots of strain or change," and helping them process how to settle on difficult choices.

"Seeing how you settle on choices is the beginning stage to settling on a progressively educated choice later on. Your remarkable basic leadership style addresses your qualities and furthermore addresses your most noteworthy shortcoming," he says. "The expectation is to encircle yourself with others that settle on choices in different styles to settle on an increasingly educated and keen decision for snapshots of strain or change. When we comprehend our styles better, we are allowed the chance to welcome others from other one of a kind points of view into our procedure."

Here is an outline of the seven basic leadership styles. You can utilize Shinabarger's five-minute appraisal instrument to all the more likely comprehend your own style.

1. Aggregate thinking

Individuals with this style normally accumulate a gathering of assessments before settling on any choice. Gathering agreement and purchase in from everybody controls each progression forward.

"These people accept profoundly in majority rules system," Shinabarger says. "They couldn't imagine anything better than to decide in favor of each choice."

2. Information driven

Hard information, particularly numbers, are the premise of these person's choices. They set aside some effort to inquire about, compose and consider before pushing ahead.

"The more data they accumulate, the better," Shinabarger says. "Numbers, research and reason direct what they do and how they choose."

3. Gut response

These chiefs depend on sentiments to settle on speedy choices. They wouldn't fret facing challenges and move unquestionably forward through life.

"Choices by these people are exceptionally passionate and are instinctually known in a matter of minutes," Shinabarger says. "They are guided by that minute and are often testing to anticipate by others."

4. Rundown approach

Individuals with this methodology just push ahead after deliberately thinking about the advantages and disadvantages of any choice. Their looked into records give them certainty and a pre-arranged way for what's to come.

"Each choice will begin with a bit of paper and a line attracted start to finish making a master and con list," Shinabarger says. "They can see things from each edge and won't pick until they have thought about each alternative."

5. Profoundly guided

Remaining nearby to God or otherworldly convictions and listening cautiously for an intelligible voice of heading is the procedure utilized by these people. Petition, isolation and retreat are their key techniques for choosing.

"Before any significant choice is made, they will remove an all-inclusive timeframe from all others to stop and think or ask about how to push ahead," Shinabarger says. "Until they have a tranquil purpose they won't proceed."

6. Story living

These people settle on choices dependent on the story they will find a good pace. They need to go to new places, attempt inconceivable things and tell the world.

"An incredible excursion is climb Mount Kilimanjaro today with three companions you met on Twitter yesterday," Shinabarger says. "They are the kind of individuals that can prop a blaze discussion up throughout the night."

7. Aloof uncertain

Individuals with this mindset are glad to push ahead with practically any choice as long as they don't need to make it. They maintain a strategic distance from struggle and pick by tailing others.

"They are truly OK with some other individual in their life settling on choices for them," Shinabarger says. "In each circumstance, decisions by others will consistently be the best choice."

Which is your style and how would you see it happening in your everyday basic leadership? Is it true that you are encircle yourself with enough of different styles of chiefs to settle on the best decisions for yourself and your organization?

The decisions you make as a business visionary can have incredible effects. The "possibility of a lifetime" can show up out of the blue just to transform into something difficult. On the other hand, there are those open doors that don't appear to be deserving of a second look at that point however inevitably wriggle their way on to your botched chance rundown. Barkeep, I think I'll have another.

You would prefer not to take advantage of simply any lucky break - you need the correct chance. All things considered, this is your valuable pioneering infant of-a thought that you need to succeed, and that implies coming around tomorrow dependent on the decision(s) you make today.

Basic leadership can be the single-most noteworthy load upon your shoulders if you don't have a clue how to oversee pressure or if the results are not exactly perfect. Anyway, how would you know what a decent choice resembles? Here are nine qualities of a decent choice:

1. Great choices emphatically sway others.

This announcement may appear glaringly evident, however if it were, terrible choices wouldn't exist. All things considered, anyone who is antagonistically influenced by a choice promptly classifies that choice as awful. Obviously, presently you simply need to locate a typical meaning of "positive."

2. Great choices are replicable.

Individuals need to emulate an awful choice like an instance of herpes. That's all anyone needs to know (and don't hesitate to tweet that).

3. Great choices encourage opportunity.

A powerful choice engages others to act.

4. Great choices incorporate others.

Coming to an end result that serves the organization is a procedure. There are boxes to mark off that guarantee accountabilities are built up and specialists are met.

5. Great choices are executable.

Fundamental to any choice is clearness around what that choice is. If there's equivocalness about what to do next then that choice isn't sufficiently clear. Clearness limits vulnerability, and despite the fact that this may seem like a conspicuous articulation, recollect that what's obvious to you might be recently discovered understanding to other people.

6. A decent choice is efficient.

Precluding the great criteria from the terrible requires time, assets, clear (there's that word once more) prerequisites about what the objective is and judgment to assess the likelihood of accomplishment.

7. Great choices are responsible.

With clearness likewise comes responsibility. It is difficult taking cover behind something that diagrams, in detail, the jobs, obligations or desires related with another choice. Attach the course of events, resources important and the conditions that characterize achievement and you're essentially on a single direction parkway to execution with no U-turns (my illustration for responsibility shirking).

8. Great choices are realistic.

People are animals of feeling, which means disposing of feeling from a choice isn't attainable. Be that as it may, what can be dispensed with are self-serving enthusiastic predispositions. In the SEAL Teams, for instance, there were three criteria whereupon choices were made: The strategic, group, the person. To be specific, who does the choice serve? Indication: The individual comes last.

When you're confronted with another difficult choice, ask yourself, "Whom does it serve?"

9. Great choices include mindfulness.

If you're entrusted with concluding how to diagram your organization's system for the following 10 years yet you've never made a key framework, odds are you ought to concede to the following topic master. The fact is, for a choice to emphatically affect others, encourage opportunity or any of the previously mentioned qualities, you should be perceptive of when you're working inside your hover of impact and when you're pushing its limits. Try not to be that individual who clasps to basic leadership authority because it causes you to feel significant - concede to the individual nearest to the issue.

Basic leadership is both a workmanship and a science. Join the over nine attributes into your decision engineering to feel progressively sure, and watch others do likewise.

As of late, a brilliant, canny official moved toward me for some exhortation. She'd began a new position and was battling with one of her acquired workers. The representative had worked for the organization for a long time, and the main thing more terrible than his presentation was his mentality.

I initially asked what she'd just attempted to take care of the issue. Her reaction was a great clothing list: she'd clarified desires, given criticism, made results and trained - all without much of any result. She had an inclination that she was out of alternatives.

I started, "Do you need my reaction in affable or direct structure?" She grinned and unhesitatingly mentioned an immediate methodology. Distrustfully, I argued, "Why in the world haven't you terminated him?!"

She disclosed to me she was stressed over being viewed as The Hatchet Lady. "In any case, she proceeded gravely, "things will be far and away more terrible if I keep him, won't they?"

I grinned. "You recognized what you expected to do before you moved toward me, didn't you?" She gestured. "Indeed, hell, you needn't bother with my recommendation! Quit pondering it and do it!" She concurred and vowed to keep me advised.

This story helped me to remember a discussion I as of late had with my companion, Chuck Blakeman. He was persistently listening me to cry about an apparently unsolvable issue. With a gleam in his eye, he energetically asked, "Tasha, what are you professing not to know?" The inquiry brought me to an abrupt halt and has since become a touchstone to soar my mindfulness.

The human mind is a unimaginable creation. It's wired to sift through data and settle on trustworthy choices dependent on impulse alone. Truth be told, when one investigation requested that members utilize their gut to choose the better of two choices, they picked accurately 90 percent of the time!

Regardless of our cerebrum's magnificent wiring, we often dismiss what's directly before us. One investigation indicated that individuals are more awful at distinguishing lies when they intentional about them as opposed to depending on their gut responses. Other work has demonstrated that when we over think choices, their quality decreases.

The vast majority will disclose to you that their gut once in a while guides them wrong. Be that as it may, we often overlook our impulses when the appropriate response is badly arranged. My companion Roger, who works in the basic food item industry, as of late revealed to me that when another contract won't work out, he knows in only a couple of days. "The issue," he noted, "is that I don't constantly like the appropriate response!"

In no way, shape or form am I immaculate at this either. I've often wound up covering reality when I should know better. Each June throughout the previous six years, I've ridden Colorado's MS150 out of appreciation for my brilliant stepdad Richard. It's a 150-mile bicycle ride to raise assets for research and treatment of different sclerosis. Paving the way to a year ago's ride, I scarcely prepared by any stretch of the imagination. I didn't have time! I supported, I'm excessively occupied with work. Lo and view, on second day of the ride, I gagged a couple of miles from the end goal so seriously that I needed to wave to the feared SAG wagon.

Stop and think for a minute: I was whimsical enough to be shocked when, where it counts, I realized this was actually what would occur. I was simply professing not to know it. Fortunately I took in my exercise and really prepared during the current year's ride, which went off easily.

I attempt to get somewhat more intelligent consistently whenever conceivable.

The lesson of this story: We live more straightforward, progressively effective lives when we quit overlooking what, where it counts, we know to be valid about ourselves and our general surroundings. Am I letting you know not to all the more profoundly think about your issues? No! I am stating that when you disregard the little voice in your mind because you don't care for what it's letting you know, you're in a hazardous area.

Building up the ideal morning schedule that augments your lifestyle and preferences - while pressing the most profitability out of your days - is an experimentation procedure. You need to realize yourself so as to modify the best morning schedule, and one size doesn't fit all. For instance: Do you need espresso to try and get into the shower? If the appropriate response is a reverberating "yes," consider incorporating it with your daily practice by setting up your espresso producer the prior night. That way, you can wake up and promptly hit the "on" switch.

Fortunately some morning "best practices" have been appeared to help fruitful business magnates and business people benefit as much as possible from their time and vitality. Investigate the following 14 slides to see which morning schedule hacks you can incorporate with your custom to assist you with sloping up efficiency and arrive at your objectives.

QUIT OVERTHINKING AND DO THE WORK

Overthinking is as weakening as it is normal. It can prevent you from getting a charge out of get-togethers, upset your rest, undermine your activity execution and even ruin your excursions. Ordinarily, constant overthinking likewise accompanies all the physical distresses of nervousness. This implies overthinking leaves you intellectually upset as well as depleted. If this image sounds well-known, you're presumably urgent to turn out how to quit overthinking your life and begin living. In any case, you may have just attempted to change and thought that it was an unfavorable obstacle.

Know that figuring out how to beat tension (and overthinking) is conceivable. Regardless of whether you're attempting to make sense of how to quit overthinking in a relationship, how to stop fanatical considering your health or how to appreciate associating without freezing, there are ground-breaking systems you can learn. We should investigate how to quit overthinking, first by characterizing the issue and afterward by taking a gander at the best arrangements.

What Is Overthinking Disorder?

Things being what they are, what precisely is overthinking disorder? We as a whole get sucked into over the top contemplations here and there, yet when this begins to devour our lives it transforms into a genuine, interminable issue. A few people are almost certain than others to endure this issue. For instance, those with a past filled with nervousness disorder. All things considered, researchers realize that overthinking enacts similar pieces of the mind that are associated with dread and tension.

In any case, regardless of whether you don't have a background marked by psychological wellness difficulties, you may be inclined to overthinking if you view yourself as an "issue solver". Your most prominent resource, an investigative personality, can without much of a stretch become a foe when you stall out in a circle of useless contemplations. Furthermore, significant levels of vulnerability can trigger the overthinking disorder. For instance, if something emotional has changed in your life or you have encountered a significant misfortune, your brain may begin to winding toward useless obsessiveness.

Overthinking Symptoms And Signs Of Anxiety

It's valuable to have an authoritative rundown of overthinking disorder indications. This permits you to identify when you are truly getting into a perilous area for your emotional wellness.

Taking a gander at the accompanying side effects can assist you with leading an overthinking disorder test.

You can't rest.

When you attempt, you can't kill your psyche, and you start to feel upset by stresses or questions.

You self-sedate.

Concentrates on overthinking disorder recommend you may go to drugs, liquor, nourishment or other outside methods for managing your feelings. This is because you don't feel ready to quiet down utilizing our inward assets.

You're constantly worn out.

This might be from sleep deprivation, or just from the consistent circle of your unsettled considerations.

You need to control everything.

You attempt to design each part of your life, down to the last detail. This is the main way you have a sense of security, however it never entirely works (because it's difficult to control everything).

You fixate on disappointment.

You will in general be a fussbudget and often envision how horrendous it is flop in any capacity. This dread of disappointment often incapacitates you, keeping you from gaining from any mix-ups.

You dread what's to come.

Rather than being energized by all you've yet to achieve and encounter, you are caught in your own nervousness about what could turn out badly.

You don't confide in your own judgment.

You re-think yourself on everything based on what you're wearing to where you're going, what you're stating and how you go over to other people. Furthermore, you may depend on others to promise you that your judgment is sound.

You get strain migraines.

These vibe like a tight band around your sanctuaries, and you may likewise see torment or stiffness in your neck. Constant strain cerebral pains are an indication that you frantically need a rest.

Free Law Of Attraction QuizFree Law Of Attraction Quiz: How Soon Will You Be Living Your Dreams And How Can You Manifest Them Faster?

Instructions to Stop Overthinking And Overcome Anxiety

Defeating over the top musings requires an activity plan. If you need to quit overthinking, you have to discover direct procedures that work, and rehash them until they become natural. You may likewise profit by treatment or therapeutic intercessions if your nervousness is particularly crippling, yet you can utilize functional activities related to these medicines.

Here are five of the most ideal approaches to defeat nervousness and shut down your persistent circle of considerations. As you become acclimated to them, you can adjust and modify them to suit you. Thus, continue perusing to find how to quit overthinking today!

5 Ways To Stop Overthinking Now

1. Know about Your Thought Process And Anxiety Triggers

the most effective method to quit overthinking

Fanatical overthinking is different for everybody, so it's crucial to know your nervousness one of a kind triggers. It assists with developing a more profound degree of consciousness of your overthinking, asking inquiries regarding for what valid reason and when it happens.

Begin giving nearer consideration to your points of view, and notice when you're thinking in an ineffective manner. Note down what you're thinking, and the structure it takes.

For instance, would you say you are replaying a past discussion on a circle, breaking down it for your disappointments?

On the other hand, would you say you are envisioning future fiasco situations in your creative mind? Moreover, compose what you think affected the overthinking. Was it something to do with a social cooperation? Vulnerability? Heading off to another condition?

Your notes will rapidly assist you with selecting specific triggers for your uneasiness. This gives you ammo to challenge the fundamental constraining convictions through reflection or diary work. In time, you will have the option to appropriate triggers before they cause a genuine scene of overthinking, mediating with a portion of the further strategies recorded underneath. In the end, the expectation is that the triggers will likewise turn out to be less incredible because you'll comprehend their starting points and expertise to retaliate in your psyche.

2. The most effective method to Stop Overthinking With These Organization Tips

Perhaps the most ideal approaches to quit overthinking is to saddle new down to earth methods for managing life's difficulties. Consider the accompanying tips specifically when attempting to figure out how to quit overthinking:

Receive a more extensive point of view. When something is annoying you, ask yourself: will this issue in a year? What about a month? What about half a month? Often, you'll see it won't make any difference even a month down the line. This can enable you to unwind.

Settle on time-constrained choices. For instance, you may allow yourself five minutes to choose about something minor (for example regardless of whether you're heading off to some housework or whether you'll go to the rec center today). In the meantime, you may take all things considered thirty minutes to choose a greater issue like whether to give an introduction or go to a major get-together.

Take breaks for the duration of the day. Decreased by and large uneasiness levels by taking standard breaks to do quieting things (for example 10 minutes of reflection, 30 minutes of perusing a fiction book or 20 minutes of strolling in the recreation center).

Limit overpowering information. It's additionally useful to set time restrains on things like working with messages, perusing online life and so on. If one of your triggers is this sort of tangible over-burden, you may allow yourself 15 minutes four times each day for these undertakings, yet no more.

3. Utilize Positive Daily Affirmations For Anxiety

Certifications are explanations that assist you with defeating negative musings. They are especially helpful if you need to figure out how to quit overthinking around evening time or need to set yourself up for an extraordinary day before anything else.

Here are some acceptable certifications for nervousness:

"I have the ability to choose what I will think about. My musings don't control me."

"At the present time, I discharge my fanatical contemplations and let them go."

"I won't permit my creative mind to show me appalling fates."

"We as a whole live right now and value the magnificence of what's going on now."

"I am more than my negative musings. I can and will be cheerful."

You can likewise structure your own positive every day attestations. There are no set guidelines for the structure they should take. Likewise, have a go at saying them into the mirror, looking straight into your own eyes. What's more, grin, if it feels normal.

4. Get Active! Retrain Your Brain To Think Positively

Figuring out how to quit overthinking, tension and anxiety additionally have a great deal to improve associations with your physical body. Both physical and mental types of positive incitement help to modify risky, negative perspectives. For instance:

Exercise can do some amazing things for the over-scholar. It concentrates the psyche on something clear, organized and fulfilling, transforming repressed vitality into something you can utilize. It likewise floods the body with feel-great endorphins that make you increasingly positive when all is said in done. Discover something you truly love, regardless of whether it's a group activity, running in a beautiful spot, cycling with companions or swimming laps after work.

Connect with your cerebrum in discovering some new information. Get another dialect, take a stab at something inventive you've never endeavored, make sense of how to play another critical thinking game (for example chess, Sudoku or Scrabble), or take up some type of making.

You can rehearse contemplation for overthinking. Basic, 10-minute body examining practices function admirably here. Inhale profoundly for a couple of moments, then think about the sensations in each piece of your body, working from head to do. Notice strain, and discharge it. On the other hand, profound breathing likewise functions admirably without anyone else. Take in through the nose for two seconds, and out through the mouth for four. This example is demonstrated to be the most unwinding.

5. Be Patient And Live In The Now

Figuring out how to quit overthinking and stressing additionally includes developing methods for better living right now. Right off the bat, don't permit yourself to be held prisoner by dubious feelings of dread about what may befall you. Rather, go up against the hardest inquiry: What is the most terrible that could occur? Often, it won't be as awful as you might suspect.

What's more, you'll commonly find you really have the assets to manage the most dire outcome imaginable. Also, use strategies that grapple you right now. When you're overthinking, slow down genuinely. Attempt to see each development of your muscles and everything around you. Your mind will slow accordingly. You can likewise have a go at portraying the present in your mind (for example "Presently I am going for a stroll. Presently I am getting dressed") to pull yourself back to the present.

Is it accurate to say that you are Ready To Overcome Anxiety And Live Your Dream Life?

At long last, work to acknowledge that you can't control everything. This is the point of your overthinking, and it's at last keeping you down. To develop and create as an individual, you have to energetically move out of your usual range of familiarity into places where the startling can occur. You additionally should have the option to gain from mix-ups and consider them to be open doors for development as opposed to as disappointments.

CONCLUSION

So suppose you're hanging about at a social affair, encompassed by associates and customers, and you have spotted somebody you truly need to converse with. Perhaps its business related or you simply need to develop individual ties. The manner in which it is, you set up a psychological draft of what to state, as one does, and plan to go meet them yet a shivering apprehension in the rear of your head leaves you speechless. Imagine a scenario in which they would prefer not to chat with you. Imagine a scenario in which the specific line of discussion doesn't work out. Or then again even turns out badly? Your dread makes a kind of domino impact, and you start to think about the most terrible that could occur as the unavoidable. With each idea you are maneuvered further into the tangled wreckage of perplexity inside your brain, and this, at last, renders you incapable to try and talk any longer. You then watch as someone else participates in a discussion with the subject: an open door lost.

Overthinking and the ensuing fretfulness and uneasiness, while ends up being an enormous hindrance in one's social and individual life, is likewise shockingly normal and for each individual who is an unfortunate casualty to it, turns into the reason for circumstances lost and minutes that one would later lament. Be that as it may, with a couple of day by day rehearses and a decided frame of mind, it very well may be defeated effectively.

The initial move towards managing inordinate overthinking and uneasiness is tolerating the issue in any case. Simply after this would you have the option to feel free to tackle it. In any case, while realizing that you are a remunerator is significant, it is additionally imperative that you understand that you are not the only one in the circumstance, and that there is no motivation to freeze. Overthinking is a typical thing among many individuals today, and you would have the option to beat it with an inspirational disposition.

The best thing you can do about overthinking is clearly to remain with the present. Your cerebrum can't consider faraway issues if it's bustling where it ought to be-with the stream. You likewise figure out how to value your environment, and being in the present totally improves your presentation on any sort of errand significantly. Furthermore, despite the fact that it is a lot more difficult than one might expect, there are a couple of techniques which you can practice day by day to limit the pattern of negative considerations all things considered.

One genuine model is relaxing. You'd be astonished at how a lot of this makes a difference. Simply close your eyes and take full breaths for two or three minutes. Intently watching and taking full breaths help to pull you in the present minute, and helps in clearing your head.

Another genuine model is contemplating to rehearse care. The fundamental thought is to stay quiet and essentially center around all that is around you intently, and this has done some amazing things for many individuals. Just once per day, simply close your eyes and attempt to take in the entirety of your environment. Tune in to your considerations however don't 'collaborate' with them, and inevitably you can attempt to cut back their 'volume'.

Notwithstanding that, slow down. Do all that you do with full consciousness of you doing it. Attempt to describe to yourself each progression that you make, and power yourself to see your environment. This will likewise assist you with staying right now.

When full to the overflow with confidence and liking yourself, you develop a positive mentality. You would end up to be less inclined to overthinking, thus everything that you do or say ends up being improved. One of the primary things you can do is get going. Structure an arrangement of what to accomplish for the afternoon, and continue being profitable. Doing things shield your psyche from straying, and notwithstanding that, completing stuff brings about an incredible lift in certainty through a feeling of achievement. You ought to likewise attempt to accomplish something you're great in any event once every day. Regardless of whether you're a specialist at playing an instrument or you have phenomenally ability for a computer game, take a break from your timetable and do it. It'll be an extraordinary assistance.

Another life adjusting transform you can make is to counterfeit it. This may sound hard however this really works extraordinary. Imagine that you're a character you know, who is clever, shrewd and certain about themselves. Maybe you know one from a network show, a motion picture or a book. Feel free to convey all that you state with certainty, regardless of whether you don't know of it, or you're terrified. You'll see that as you counterfeit it to an ever increasing extent, in the long run, you acquire that trust, all things considered.

Attempting to control all the results of your life is without a doubt the fundamental driver for compensation. Because when you do, you are likewise bound to hotly consider what to do in each snapshot of your life in dread of what could therefore occur straightaway. The best thing you can do is to persuade yourself not to. Understand that you have nothing to do with what occurs in your life, and this there is no motivation to stress over it. The universe has your destiny chosen, so you should simply make the most out of each minute. Attempt to understand this before anything you may be dithering to do, and it'll assist you with stopping overthinking and take care of business.

Something else you can do make specific time allotments to settle on any choice. Regardless of whether it is to proceed to converse with somebody, or greater life decisions which may be constraining you to overthinking. Pause for a moment for the little ones and a couple of days for the bigger ones in life and no more. This would push you to evaluate a choice sanely and research to settle on the most ideal decision. When you do settle on a choice, steel yourself and take care of business. It may be terrifying yet you'll see it compensating toward the end.

CPSIA information can be obtained
at www.ICGtesting.com
Printed in the USA
BVHW081428121120
593172BV00015B/1432

9 781913 978150